ALCOHOLISM

ALCOHOLISM

How to Deal With a Drink Problem

by
Freddy C.

THORSONS PUBLISHING GROUP

First published 1976
Revised and expanded edition 1988

© FREDDY C. 1976

British Library Cataloguing in Publication Data

C. Freddy
Alcoholism: how to deal with a drink problem.
1. Alcoholism
I. Title II. C. Freddy. Alcohol problem explained
362.2'92   HV5035

ISBN 0-7225-1618-5

*Published by Thorsons Publishers Limited, Wellingborough,
Northamptonshire, NN8 2RQ, England*

Printed in Great Britain by Woolnough Bookbinding
Limited, Irthlingborough, Northamptonshire

1 3 5 7 9 10 8 6 4 2

CONTENTS

FOREWORD

Some people say Jimmy Greaves was an alcoholic. That is incorrect. I am an alcoholic.

The popular view of the alcoholic is some poor old guy under a railway bridge with a bottle of meths, but the majority of alcoholics are not like that.

The illness can hit anyone, anywhere in the world. It has no boundaries and is no respecter of a person or reputation.

Unfortunately nonalcoholics have no real conception of the illness, so books like Freddy's serve two vitally important purposes.

Alcoholics will identify with it and it will help put them or keep them on the road to recovery. Like a man who loses a leg has to learn to walk again, so the alcoholic has to rebuild his life.

For nonalcoholics, Freddy's experiences can provide a wider understanding of a problem which even the medical profession is sometimes frightened of.

Read the book. The chances are it will help you — or help you help someone you know.

JIMMY GREAVES

PREFACE

This book has been written for those who have, or think they may have, a drink problem.

It has also been written for the families, friends and colleagues of such persons, for they, just as much as the drinker, suffer from what is arguably the most distressing illness known to man.

A great many people, especially in the medical profession, have devoted many years to the study of alcoholism and the alcoholic and the writer of this book would like to pay a sincere tribute to their efforts.

But doctors, hypnotists and psychiatrists have had but limited success in the treatment of this particular condition, a condition which, after coronaries and cancer is the third of the world's 'killer' illnesses. Without doubt, the greatest source of help to the problem drinker and to those closest to them is a knowledge of the illness from which they *all* suffer.

It should be noted that when the words 'he' or 'man' are used in this book, the words 'she' and 'woman' are equally applicable. Alcohol certainly has no respect for the sexes. But who are the experts in this field? Who can talk or write with any great authority on a subject which is as complex as it is baffling? Many claim, with some justification, that they have such a right, and the writer of this book would in no way argue with their claims. But there can be no doubt that the person who is as entitled as any to proffer help on this subject is the alcoholic who has managed to *stop* drinking, has managed to *stay* stopped, and has devoted his years of sobriety to a study of the illness from which he once suffered. The writer of this book is such a person and he offers the following pages in the sincere hope that the reader will find in them that which he himself has been fortunate enough to find — happy sobriety.

1.

NATURE'S ANAESTHETIC

The stuff has been around a long time now. Turn to Genesis 9:20-21 and you will find that the man we have to blame (or praise) for it all was the old master mariner himself, Noah. The said verses read: 'And Noah began to be an husbandman, and he planted a vineyard: and he drank of the wine, and was drunken; and he was uncovered within his tent.'

So there you have it; Noah, the first of the many who have had good cause to either bless or curse the effects of drinking too much alcohol. And if, on that morning after the night before, Noah uttered those immortal words 'Never again', then the chances are that he had learned his lesson and that his drinking would in future have been confined to that for which it was primarily intended: social occasions. But if, on that fateful morning, Noah reached for the vino bag with trembling hands and took a swig along with the fervent promise 'Just one for the road', then it may well be that Noah was not only the first of the world's drinkers, but also the first of the world's problem drinkers.

It is indeed doubtful if any other product has caused more merriment, tears, laughter, hatred, *bonhomie* or family feuds than our old friend, alcohol.

Poets have written about it:

> John Barleycorn was a hero hold,
> Of noble enterprise;
> For if you do but taste his blood,
> 'Twill make your courage rise.
> (Robert Burns)

Songs have been sung about it (For); sermons have been preached about it (Against), and it has had probably the greatest advertising campaign in history conducted on its behalf. It now has a sophistication that transcends the humble grape juice sampled by Noah; and for something that excites, calms, enlivens, soothes, warms or cools, it has no equal.

It is inconceivable that the legions of Caesar would have marched without an adequate supply of the stuff (nor did they); and it is equally inconceivable that the ships of Drake or Nelson set sail without ample quantities of it (and they didn't). And if some unfortunate legionnaire or sailor had had the misfortune to require the amputation of a limb, then alcohol assumed yet another role — that of literal anaesthetic. The victim would drink it to bring about that blessed oblivion that would enable the surgeon to set about his gruesome task. Not for nothing has it been called nature's anaesthetic, and for those who can handle it, it has indeed been a blessing, a comfort and an ally.

But for those who can't handle it . . . .

What Makes an Alcoholic?

It would be simplicity itself to say that if a person cannot handle alcohol — they shouldn't drink it! But this type of simple logic is lost upon those who derive — or once derived — comfort from alcohol. So, at this point three questions present themselves:

1. Who is an alcoholic?
2. Why is it that two people can drink the same amount of alcohol and yet only one of them becomes an alcoholic?
3. Is it only alcohol that creates the alcoholic, or is there some 'hidden' factor?

There have been many answers to the first question, and as good an answer as any would be: One who has lost the power to control his drinking.

It is a fact that few drinking alcoholics or problem drinkers would accept that they have lost the power to control their drinking habits. One of the most famous of all drinking aphorisms is: I can take it or leave it — so I take it!

But, of course, the only way to prove that one can take it or leave it *is to leave it now and then.*

The problem drinker prides (or deludes) himself on the fact that he can stop drinking any time he wants to. It is only because he doesn't want to stop that he keeps on. A strange logic, and one that is well-known to recovering alcoholics.

The Power of Choice

The great difference between the alcoholic drinker and the social (light, moderate or heavy) drinker is the fact that if the social drinker *wanted* to give up drinking, he could. The reason for this is that he still has the power of choice. But the alcoholic drinker has lost this power, and even if he wanted to quit drinking, he just couldn't. He may, of course, stop for long periods, but there is always this strange power that seems to beckon him towards the first drink, and once that first drink has been taken, it is only a matter of time (usually a short period) before the alcoholic has resumed his former drinking pattern.

There is nothing sadder than the alcoholic drinker trying desperately to drink as he once did, without the consequences of his drinking. Alcoholism, like obesity, is unique in the fact that it is, or can be, quite pleasant in its early stages. The victim may drink for a variety of reasons, and booze can very effectively serve its purpose. The man who is shy and reticent and who, on taking a drink, suddenly finds himself full of self-confidence and strength would find it difficult indeed to believe that alcohol is his enemy. He has found a new friend in booze and cannot — will not — believe that anything could ever break up this now inseparable pair. And man and alcohol have been an inseparable pair for a very long time now. Remember Noah?

The second question posed — why is it that two people can drink the same amount of alcohol and yet only one of them becomes an alcoholic? — is fairly simple — if disappointing — to answer . . . we just do not know. It may well be that science or medical research will one day present us with the answer as to what chemical change takes place in the body of the alcoholic, but not in the body of the social drinker, when both drink alcohol. But, to date, no answer has been forthcoming. A tremendous amount of research is being made into this aspect of the illness in an attempt to find an answer, the point being that if the chemical change that takes place (if, in fact, such a change does take place) can be discovered, then some means may be found of combating this change. If this were possible it could mean that the alcoholic drinker might be able to revert to social drinking. Many, many thousands of suffering alcoholics are praying for this happy day to arrive when they will be able to drink without the consequences of their drinking.

Total Abstinence

All those concerned in the treatment of alcoholism are more than agreed that the only way for the alcoholic to overcome the *physical* craving for alcohol is total abstinence. This also applies to the heroin addict. The only way for him to combat the awful obsession for his drug is to keep away from the stuff as far as possible. But heroin and alcohol are two entirely different drugs, taken for entirely different reasons (though both have the same addictive hold over the users), and it is here that alcoholism is more complex than any other drug addiction.

No one suggests that heroin is ever taken for 'social' reasons. When a person takes the 'hard' drugs, they do so (whether they know it or not) with the gravest suspicion cast upon their motives for doing so. But alcohol is invariably taken in the first instance as a social extra; and it is from this seemingly innocuous beginning that the seeds for future danger fruits are planted.

The first pint of bitter at the village pub gives no indication that the drinker has — or may have — taken his first steps on the way to Skid Row. The first small sherry sipped by the lady at the theatre bar in no way conjures up a picture of that same lady hiding bottles of sherry all over the house. And a drop of brandy 'for medicinal purposes' was never meant to lead to a situation where that brandy (or any other drink) would become the most important commodity in the drinker's life.

If you take heroin then you expect big trouble. But if you take alcohol, you don't expect any trouble at all — except maybe a sore head on waking the next morning. What you definitely don't expect is a *physical* compulsion to drink, drink and drink; and even when you don't drink, a *mental* obsession that drives you inexorably towards the first one.

Is There a Hidden Factor?

And so to the third question: Is it only alcohol that creates the alcoholic, or is there some 'hidden' factor? Of the three questions, this one is the most difficult to answer.

Remember what was said about the man who, on taking his favourite tipple, suddenly found himself free from his fears, doubts and inadequacies? Once that kind of transformation has taken place, a bond has been formed between the drinker and that which is drunk, and it is a more than difficult bond to break. Some people do not want to break it, and without this desire, in a great many cases it simply cannot be broken.

If a man thinks that alcohol gives him a certain 'thing' that cannot be achieved in any other way, then all the lectures, homilies and sermons to the contrary will have little or no effect upon him. What he needs is a substitute for alcohol, and until he gets it his liaison with booze is a very strong one. But is there a substitute for alcohol? Can anything give him the glow and the self-confidence that alcohol gives, or gave, him?

Experiments have been made by the thousand in an effort to find the magic formula. Pills by the million have been prescribed to try and do the trick. Valium and Librium tablets by the hundreds of millions have been swallowed in a vain effort to recapture the 'that's better' feeling that once came with the first drink. In some cases it has worked — but only as a temporary expedient. In a very short time the alcoholic who has substituted pills for booze is back on the old merry-go-round. Only this time it's tablets he is taking to excess instead of alcohol.

Again we come to the point that seems to run throughout the whole field of the drinking alcoholic: awareness of the illness from which he suffers, the total dependence he now has for alcohol, and a willingness to make the world of reality and mature thinking his substitute for booze.

That, of course, means a complete, albeit slow, change from the man that he *is* to the man that he *can be*. It is in this field that the 'hidden' factor is seen to be in need of discovery.

2.

THE SOCIAL DRINKER

The term 'social drinker' is in itself a fairly comforting one. It conjures up, as we have said, a pint at the village pub, a sherry at the theatre bar, or a 'hot toddy' to help keep the cold at bay. A great many people do drink in this fashion, and it is seldom that much harm befalls them, at least as far as their drinking is concerned.

Light Social Drinking
Such people can, for the purpose of category, be termed 'light' social drinkers, and from all the great numbers who do drink like this, they are the least likely to suffer either from the effects or the consequences of drinking alcohol.

The 'odd pint' at the local not only precludes any dangers of physical or mental damage to the drinker, it actually carries with it a certain *bonhomie*, for the drinker can not only enjoy a drink with his friends, he can enjoy it in a reasonable and responsible manner. The fact that alcohol adds to the enjoyment of the occasion shows that the 'light' social drinker has indeed the best of both worlds. He can 'take it or leave it', and in taking it, it adds some pleasure to his life without any undue consequences.

But if for one reason or another he *had* to give up drinking alcohol, he could do so without any difficulty whatsoever. And if he found that he missed the company of his mates at the local pub one Sunday lunchtime, he would still be able to go along there and enjoy the atmosphere of it all — only this time he would have a soft drink instead of his usual pint. He would not feel 'left out of it' just because he couldn't drink alcohol; nor would he feel in any way inferior to his friends because of the changed circumstances. He would accept the change as necessary and adjust accordingly. And the lady who *had* to stop drinking alcohol could still enjoy her visits to the theatre, accompany her companion to the theatre bar, and settle for a tomato juice. She would suffer no sense of 'loss' because of this: who knows, it may well be that she in fact prefers the tomato juice, and only drank the sherry because it was the 'accepted' thing to do. As for the person who *had* to substitute a glass of hot milk for the previous 'hot toddy', he would make the transition without any problems.

So, although these 'light' social drinkers may own up to the fact that they did enjoy their occasional tipple, the main point is that they had no overwhelming desire to have a drink, and, if need be, they would accept without reservation that their drinking days were over. Whether they drank or not was of no consequence to them, and alcohol, while being a pleasant 'extra' in their lives, was by no means a 'must'. This type of drinker really can 'take it or leave it', and if he must leave it — so be it!

Moderate Social Drinking

If light social drinking is the 'odd one' now and again, then the next stage in the drinker's progress comes under the heading of 'moderate' social drinking; that means the 'odd ones' (plural) at more frequent intervals. The term 'now and again' would hardly suffice for the pattern that is now emerging from one who can take it or leave it — and decides to take it.

The field is now widened somewhat, for if the light social drinkers can be numbered in millions, the moderates can be numbered in tens of millions.

A great many people have good cause to be grateful to the drinkers who take their favourite tipple in moderation, for if they were to revert to the 'light' social drinking stage the economy of the country would be thrown into chaos. For a start, the Chancellor of the Exchequer would have his advisors in at the double, seeking desperately to find new ways in which to recoup the missing millions of pounds that were formerly brought in by the tax on alcohol; while the brewers' and distillers' companies would themselves probably take to drink at the thought of the havoc caused to their more than lucrative businesses by the devastating drop in the revenue. Pubs and off-licences in their thousands would be out of business, along with their corresponding tenants, managers and staff; while hotels and restaurants would have to treble their menu prices to compensate for the disastrous drop in booze takings. And it is doubtful if the

Scottish economy could exist for long if its main export were now to be drunk for medicinal purposes only. Booze is big business, and the thought of any drastic change in the drinking (less) habits of the nation would cause as much of a headache at Westminster as it would at any of the aforementioned places of comfort. But, of course, there will be no drastic change in the nation's drinking habits (unless it is to drink more). There are no signs that the moderate drinkers intend drinking any less. They keep up their good, steady average; and if they (the drinkers) are happy with the arrangement, the same must be said for the brewers, pubs, etc. All are happy with an arrangement that harms no one; and when you have a situation whereby both parties — suppliers and supplied — are satisfied with that situation, then it is only right that they be allowed to exercise their privilege.

Heavy Social Drinking

But if everyone is happy with the social drinker who can handle the stuff without any adverse effects or consequences, not everyone is happy with the drinker who *cannot* handle the stuff and who *does* suffer from the effects and consequences of his drinking. The trouble here is that it is not only the drinker who suffers from the fact that he overdoes it at times; family, friends and colleagues alike are drawn into the net of suffering created by the drinker who drinks too much.

The drinker who drinks too much, and makes a habit of drinking too much, must, without doubt, be termed a 'problem' drinker. It may well be that the problem drinker is not an alcoholic, for there is indeed a difference between the two. But excessive drinking by anyone, unless he or she lives alone on a desert island, must create some form of problem not only for themselves but for those around them.

What is the difference between the problem drinker and the alcoholic? We again come back to the old saying: 'I can take it or leave it.' For the heavy drinker, even when his drinking is creating problems, the word 'or' is still the operative word. He can take it or leave it, and the fact that he *chooses* to take it means that it is indeed his *choice*. But the drinking alcoholic no longer has that power of choice. Once the first drink has been taken, the power of choice has gone, and neither he nor anyone else can guarantee his subsequent behaviour. Unless, of course, it is to take a safe bet that he will carry on drinking!

It would be true to say that if an alcoholic could exercise control over his drinking, he wouldn't be an alcoholic. So the operative words so far as the alcoholic is concerned are 'loss of control'. And that is as good a description of the alcoholic as any: one who has lost the power to control his drinking.

When a drinker loses control of his drinking, it shows in two ways: physically and mentally. And while the physical side of it is not all that difficult to spot, it is the mental change, or personality change, that can be baffling to the observer. Probably the greatest example of a personality change was portrayed in Robert Louis Stevenson's *Doctor Jekyll and Mister Hyde*. Here was the supreme example of what happens when one loses control and allows the other side of the nature to manifest.

It can be a frightening experience and it would seem that there is a Mister Hyde inside every Doctor Jekyll on this earth: there can be no doubt that alcohol brings forth Mister Hyde better than almost any other product.

Seldom, if ever, is Mister Hyde let loose by the 'light' social drinker, and the moderate drinker doesn't have all that much to worry about on that score either. The heavy drinker can soon find out if there are any personality changes when he drinks. All he has to do is ask those closest to him; they will soon tell him if he is honest in his desire for the truth. But an alcoholic drinker without a personality change is almost unknown.

If those who think that they might be alcoholics doubt this assertion — let them ask their nearest and dearest.

3.

THE ALCOHOLIC

We are now in a different league entirely; a league in which the words 'social drinking' and 'control' are only used to recall days gone by.

Millions have tried (including the writer) and no doubt millions will continue to try (but, hopefully, not the writer) to recapture the halcyon days when booze was drunk without any adverse effects, and John Barleycorn was looked upon as an old friend, a comforter and an ally for all occasions.

To the alcoholic, those days have gone! The trouble is to try and convince him of that fact. Sometimes it is only pain and anguish that will convince him that he can no longer drink; and some even go to the grave still proclaiming that 'this time it will be different'.

An Illness or Disease?

The words 'illness' and 'disease' have been used to try to describe this most complex and baffling condition, and there can be no doubt that at times no other terms will suffice. But to many people the word 'illness' or 'disease' is unacceptable, as they cannot see just how a person, having had one drink, finds it impossible to leave it at that. Can it in any way be compared to an illness such as, say, cancer? In the context of cancer, the answer must be no. Cancer can be seen. It can be detected by both X-ray and blood tests. But this is not the case with the alcoholic. The condition cannot be detected by any form of tests, and it is only apparent when the drinker actually drinks, and it is seen that he cannot stop drinking.

The man who is carried unconscious into a hospital suffering from alcoholism can, within days, show no traces of the illness, and provided there has been no physical damage such as cirrhosis of the liver, no test in the world can distinguish him from a teetotaller. Once the good doctors have pumped him full of the necessary vitamins that the booze has destroyed, he is (physically speaking) as good as new.

The Thinking Problem

But though he may be as good as new in the physical sense, in the mental sense he is in greater danger than ever. If the alcoholic does not have treatment for the *thinking* problem, the chances are that he will drink again. And it will not be long before it is apparent that the illness is not only a severe one but is also a progressive one. In other words, it gets worse.

As we have said, alcoholism, in common with obesity, can be quite enjoyable in the early stages.

The alcoholic who wakes up in the morning with just a touch of the 'shakes' would indeed find it hard to believe that the first drink of the day, which, in some magical way takes away the shakes, is some sort of an enemy. He sees that first glass as not only a necessary ally, but as a welcome one. And the alcoholic who feels a mite nervous before attempting some particular task — whether it be a business interview or asking a girl for a dance — could hardly be expected to subscribe to the proposition that the drink that filled him so full of confidence was really a deadly adversary out to destroy him. How can this be when all he feels is a sense of well-being?

The same applies to the lady who gets that same feeling of well-being from a slice of cream cake! She eats not because she is hungry, but because she has a need for the food.

It would take something far stronger than reasoned arguments to convince them that both the food and the drink are supplying a need which eventually, sooner or later, will turn into a full-scale craving.

Again it must be said that, in most cases, it is only the sheer misery of their condition that eventually forces them to seek help. It would also be true to say that what the compulsive eater and drinker seek at their first attempts to 'straighten themselves out' is not so much to be 'cured' of their compulsion, but how to eat and drink without the inevitable problems that come with their compulsion.

A Feeling of Shame

The affinity between obesity and alcoholism is also apparent when the word 'shame' is discussed, for few people can suffer more shame than the compulsive drinker and the compulsive eater. The girl who eats because she 'has to' feels shame at the grotesque figure now developing; and the more shame she feels the more she eats. One feeds upon the other, and it is one of the most vicious of circles.

The alcoholic is in exactly the same boat. He starts to feel shame, remorse, resentment and all the other emotions that come with his excessive drinking, and one of the best and most effective ways he knows to enable him to 'escape' from all those feelings is — more booze. So, he drinks to escape the problems that are complementary to his drinking, and the more he escapes the more he is trapped. As vicious a circle as the obese person is in, except that, in addition, the alcoholic who is drinking releases the Mister Hyde that is not normally apparent in the compulsive eater. While both illnesses will eventually kill the victim, there is no doubt, of the two, alcoholism is a more deadly and distressing complaint. It is sad to relate that more people on this earth are suffering from the effects of drinking too much than are suffering from the effects of eating too much.

No Permanent Cure

In this chapter the words 'sober alcoholic' have been used, and it may be that many will wonder how one can be sober and still be an alcoholic. In describing an alcoholic as 'one who has lost the power to control his drinking', it should be remembered that, to date, this loss of control can never be regained. So, even if an alcoholic has not had a drink for, say, ten years, if he were to start drinking alcohol again, his loss of control would show in a short time — sooner rather than later. Thousands of alcoholics have tried to prove this theory wrong and all have paid the cost in full.

In a way it is like the heroin addict who somehow or other manages to get off the stuff and stay off for a long time. But if he should, at some future date, decide to try 'just one more fix', then those who know the person concerned can but wait for the trouble that is sure to come.

It is not unnatural to think that if an alcoholic has not taken booze for a long time, then somehow or other the 'slate is clean' and that his time off the stuff has in some magical way enabled him to drink like he used to. He is fit and full of vitamins. He is 'aware' that he must now exercise control, and must not get into the terrible scrapes he got into in the past. This time he will take every care to see that he does not overdo it, doesn't disgrace himself, and does none of the things that he did when he was an irresponsible drinker. Armed with his length of sobriety, his awareness of the situation, and his determination to 'drink like a gentleman', our hero sets off on his new life of 'controlled social drinking' — and experience has shown that, while it is a fascinating exercise in the study of the 'returning alcoholic', the fascination is somewhat dimmed by the knowledge that his chances of achieving his goal are less than the proverbial snowball in hell.

So the sober alcoholic who attempts a 'comeback' is suffering from the cardinal delusion that somehow or other he has regained control. This can truly be termed the 'magnificent obsession' of the ex-tippler! How to drink and get away with it? If someone can come up with an answer, and one that works, they will be millionaires overnight! The demand for their remedy will be sought after in almost every country in the world. Statues will be erected in their memory from grateful drinkers who can once again indulge in their favourite pastime without waking with shakes, screaming spouses, blackouts, writs, summonses and all the rest of the paraphernalia that goes with the alcoholic drinker.

It is said that a baby is being born every few seconds of the day and night on this earth of ours. It can also be said that in those same few seconds an alcoholic is taking a drink, wishing he could take a drink, or desperately seeking a way whereby he can take a drink with no subsequent problems. But, of course, not all alcoholics run to the same pattern. The rich alcoholic may be drinking in his luxurious home, and have no screaming spouse, no writs or summonses, etc. But there is one thing for sure; if he carries on drinking, there is trouble ahead. And the once proud housewife who is sipping her sherry in the solitude of her own home may also have no screaming spouse (he may have gone!), writs or summonses, but if she carries on drinking, her problems are as painful as those of the rich alcoholic in his mansion. A raging toothache is in no way diminished because the sufferer is staying at the Savoy Hotel.

Powers of Delusion
It is true to say that the alcoholic with money can drink a better class of whisky, but this is a dubious advantage, especially when one considers that he is now allergic to the stuff. But, again, we come back to the old problem: how to convince a person that

they have lost control over booze. Remember what has been said about alcohol and its powers of delusion. Few indeed are the alcoholics who will say at the start of the problem: 'I have lost control, therefore I had better stop now while the going is reasonably good.' At that stage the stuff is 'working' for him. It is doing that for which it is being drunk, and as long as the drinker feels that booze is on his side, all the logic in the world will fail to persuade him that he has a problem. So, is all lost? The answer is quite simply No. If all were lost, this book would not have been written. And if you, the reader, thought that all was lost, the chances are that you would not be reading it now. But first let us try an experiment. It does, of course, concern booze — the drinking of and the not drinking of!

Alcoholics in their millions have gone through every test in the book to try and find the answer to controlled drinking. It must be said straightaway that they have, in the early stages of their experimentation, had varying degrees of success. For example, the alcoholic who has been released from hospital where he has had treatment for his drinking — and this could be under the heading of 'nerves', 'pressure of work', and a dozen other euphemistic terms — may, on deciding to resume his drinking habits, do so with one overriding assertion: this time it will be different. For a start he will try to look at the thing logically and see exactly where he went wrong the last time. He will probably find that he didn't eat as he should have done, and that the booze was invariably being poured into an empty stomach; so, this time he will see to it that he has a good breakfast every morning. With food inside him, the chances of him drinking too much are somewhat diminished. After all, he knows only too well that once food has been taken, the desire for a drink is lessened — albeit temporarily. He also reflects that the early morning drinking — a couple of large ones to start the day right — was in some ways the start of his downfall. So, there is again a firm resolve on his part that those early morning drinks are a thing of the past, and that from now on he will drink only during 'opening hours', plus maybe a few when he gets home from his daily job. All this sounds good in theory; after all, is this not how most of his colleagues drink? And they never seem to have the problems that he had, at least through their drinking.

Two Important 'Musts'
So, for the alcoholic drinker who wishes to resume 'social

drinking' there are two very important musts: firstly, he must see to it that he never drinks on an empty stomach, and secondly, he must only drink at 'acceptable' times. He probably knows, too, that his former overdoing it led to certain vitamin deficiencies, so this time he will take his daily dose of the required pills to see that he is indeed in top physical condition. And one other very important point: as drinking is purely a social habit, he must make certain that his social drinking is done within a framework of an acceptable social background. In other words, he will never drink alone.

And so, this time, things really will be different. The mistakes of the past will most decidedly not be repeated. But there is a snag (isn't there always!). And the snag is that all these good intentions are made *before* our hero takes a drink. And thereby hangs a tale, because once the first drink has gone down — at least, for the alcoholic — all the good intentions in the world are merely just that: good intentions. Good intentions are rather like 'best laid schemes' — and we know what Robert Burns had to say about them!

It is not the fault of the alcoholic that his intentions come to nothing. He *means* well. But alcohol is the world's great deluder, especially to those who can no longer control it. No one tries harder than an alcoholic to try and recapture the control he once had. If marks for 'trying' were to be awarded, our 'comeback' drinker would get ten out of ten. But, alas, there are no marks for trying; there is only trouble ahead. It is a fact that if an alcoholic has had a spell off the stuff, plus the fact that he is in somewhat better shape physically than he has been for a while, and is eating reasonably well, he may be able to drink with some degree of 'control' for a little time. The length of time varies; some drink in a 'sensible' manner for several months, while others are back on the old band-wagon in a matter of days. In many cases the former pattern changes and a new type of drinker emerges, but it is only a matter of time before the loss of control becomes apparent and the alcoholic is once again the sad, pathetic sight that family, friends and colleagues (if there are any left) know only too well.

The Periodic Drinker

This type of drinker has difficulty in ever thinking that he may have a problem because, as he may well say, he doesn't drink every day. In fact, this type may only drink two or three times a year. But *when he does* . . .

So it becomes apparent that it is not so much what one drinks, or when, but what it does to you. If a person only drinks two or three times a year, but during those bouts finds that he loses the power of control, he is in the same position as the drinker who drinks regularly and who also loses the power of control. The only difference is that one has longer between bouts.

Many indeed are the drinkers who never touch the stuff for months on end, and then decide to 'have a taste'. The troubles, rows, arrests and disasters that beset the periodic problem drinker are just as effective as those of his more 'regular' brother or sister.

4.

THE FEMALE ALCOHOLIC

There are not many people who would deny the fact that the suffering alcoholic — especially when getting near the end of the line — is one of the most embarrassing and pathetic sights on this earth.

But if you make it the *female* alcoholic, then that makes the situation even more embarrassing and pathetic. There are theories and statistics galore concerning women drinkers, but in this day of equal rights all theories and statistics are having to be changed; for as more and more women have a job outside the home and have their own income, more and more women are drinking; and the number of women alcoholics is slowly but surely catching up on their male counterparts.

More Women Than Ever

The number of women alcoholics having treatment for the illness in either private nursing homes or special clinics is now greater than ever. Many reasons have been advanced for this increase, and a lot of these have a certain validity. The fact that women now have more opportunities to compete with men in many fields means that they also have more pressures. And more pressures mean that more methods will be tried to combat these pressures. And we know, of course, that our old friend booze helps combat pressures better than most things. Again, in this day of equality, it is easier for the woman drinker to indulge in a habit which seems to bring certain comforts. It is not all that long since a woman would not have been allowed in a pub unless accompanied by a man. But those days have gone, and if a woman wants to drink alone in a bar, restaurant or club, then the opportunity is there.

If a woman feels any embarrassment at drinking alone publicly, she can easily buy her favourite tipple from the nearest supermarket. The access to booze is now simpler than ever, and a lady buying a bottle of sherry or vodka at a store causes no more comment than the announcing of the price!

Alcohol as a Substitute

So, if more women are drinking, it is not surprising that the number of women alcoholics is increasing, and this would seem to suggest that the increased number is simply an indication of physical addiction. The more who drink, the more are 'hooked'. But women do show one tendency to drink for a specific reason that is not so apparent in their male counterparts: as a substitute for a husband, lover, children or friends.

The number of women who drink because they are 'lonely' is well known to all who take an active interest in the illness of alcoholism, and it is when alcohol is taken as a substitute for people that you usually get the 'lonely housewife' type of drinker, sitting at home with the bottle fulfilling the role of those who are no longer around.

The housewife who is alone all day may turn to the 'odd' sherry merely to pass an otherwise boring day; and when booze is taken for this reason there is trouble ahead! The mother whose children are grown-up and no longer dependent on her may also have the odd glass to keep her company and to reassure her that she is still 'needed' in the world. She, too, is taking booze for reasons *other* than social. And if a woman feels that she has been denied the company of husband and children, and that she has left it a bit late to indulge in the company of a lover — well, the bottle can be as good a substitute for those 'absent companions' as any other.

The woman who drinks for those reasons embraces a bottle of alcohol with the same fervour as a Juliet embraces her Romeo. The stimulating company that the husband used to provide can be had at the turn of a bottle top. Instant company, instant stimulus, and instant friend. It eases aching hearts as well as aching muscles. It befriends with an all-enveloping embrace that relieves not only tired limbs but also a weary soul.

Instant Companionship

Where there was loneliness, there is now companionship. And where there was the feeling of being 'unwanted', there is now the awareness that booze will never let down those who believe all it promises; promises that are given with the fervour and sincerity of a saint.

The real snag, of course, is that the promises *are* kept, albeit for only a time. But during the time they are kept and the bottle *does* provide instant friendship and warmth, it would take more than words — whether written or spoken — to convince the drinker that she is the victim of a big 'con' trick. History is littered with the victims of Casanova and his type, who wave their magic wands in the pursuit of love and who leave in their wake a line of broken hearts.

But while the sad and sorrowful victims of Casanova were at least eventually rid of the charming and plausible seducer, the same cannot be said for those who embrace alcohol to their bosom. He doesn't go easily. Not for him a parting of the ways when the body has been conquered: he wants the mind as well. And it is sad to relate that when he has destroyed both body and mind, they are discarded with a ruthlessness that is seldom seen in any other field of operation.

The 'Lonely Illness'

Alcoholism has often been referred to as the 'lonely illness', and it is true to state that a greater number of women alcoholics suffer alone than do male alcoholics. This is by the very nature of things. Where the male alcoholic will, at least for a time, be accepted and/or tolerated, the female alcoholic will be neither accepted nor tolerated. And so she is forced to do her drinking, or at least the greater part of it, at home.

This causes problems which are peculiar to the female. The suffering female alcoholic may have children who are dependent on her, and the struggle to keep up a pretence that all is well is an almost impossible task. The fact that many do it, and for a fair length of time, shows a trait in the human character that is not apparent in any other species. They *have to* keep going, and they do. Children are seen to and then sent to school, and then it is time for a welcome drink. Then the shopping must be done, and then another drink. Then maybe a sleep. But the house must be tidied before the man arrives home. Dinner must be prepared — and the empties must be got rid of. And all this must be carried out with the bland assurance that all is well. If there are money problems because of the drinking, they must be explained away with the minimum of fuss. It may be that she also has to be a wife in every sense of the word to her husband, and this is no easy task when the one thing uppermost on her mind is the next drink.

Trying to Hide the Facts

Can the children's talk *really* be important to her when she is desperately trying to appear normal, trying to suppress the slight shakes that may be beginning, and trying to hide the fact that certain bills have not been paid? When she is told she is 'letting herself go' both physically and mentally, and the remarks from either husband, children or friends are made with a cutting venom that goes deep within her, and leaves scars that do not heal, there is always one who she can turn to for comfort, one she can turn to for support and one she can turn to for understanding: alcohol.

Again it is asked to do a certain job, and it complies very well — for a time. And the woman who has no children to consider may drink throughout the day to combat the loneliness of the home, and then try to sober up for the arrival of the working husband. This, too, can be done for a certain length of time, but desperate indeed are the women who at last realize that their old friend booze is beginning to turn. They want rid of him, but he won't go. And if he did go, he leaves such a 'miss' in the house that he is virtually irreplaceable. It really is Hobson's choice for them. Hell with him, or Hell without him. Can there be any sadder sight than the female alcoholic who can't live with him, and can't live without him? Again we come to the fact that in some way or another, booze must be replaced by something else.

A woman who has come to depend utterly on alcohol for her every need, must have something very powerful indeed to replace it. Is there anything? Again, the answer is Yes — and it is nearer than you think.

5.

THE YOUNG ALCOHOLIC

Which is worse, the female or the male alcoholic? The choice is indeed an unenviable one. The man who in the past has been a loving and considerate husband and father, is a frightening and bewildering sight to behold as he changes from his former self into the person who is in the grip of alcoholism. His changes of mood, perhaps violence, loss of work, lack of consideration and complete inability to do anything about it (other than the promises) are hard to bear for the family who expected so much more.

The woman who, in the past, was a loving and considerate wife and mother is a sad and sorry object to those who once loved her for the person she was. The lies and excuses are now unacceptable to all concerned; and a father who comes home to a house that has as its keeper a practising alcoholic is indeed to be pitied. For not only has he a house to see to, he may also have a young family dependent upon him for their emotional needs. He, too, must play a dual role, and it is to their credit that so many husbands of alcoholics play this role as well as they do.

But if it is a sad and sorry sight to have either husband or wife who is drinking, it is an even more sad and sorry sight when it involves a young person. At one time, and not so long ago, the incidence of teenage drinkers was not all that much of a problem. For one thing, it was not esay for the under-age drinker to get hold of the stuff. He couldn't drink in bars, clubs or restaurants (unless, of course, he looked a lot older than he was), and he couldn't walk into off-licences and just order what he wanted. There was a law that precluded him from consuming it on licensed premises, and so if alcoholism was going to afflict that particular person it would be at a later age, i.e. once he had done his fair share of 'social' drinking.

Greater Emotional Need

But when you get cases of teenagers whose drinking is out of
control, it shows that if they have done any social drinking at
all, it must have been at an extremely early age for them to be
'hooked' in their teens. It also shows that there is a much greater
emotional need in this type of young alcoholic than in his older
counterpart, for where the older drinker has usually had a long
period of time to become physically and mentally dependent on
alcohol, the young drinker has dropped into this sad state in but
a short space of time.

If anything good can be said about this kind of drinker, it is
that, providing he wants help and is willing to go along with the
various kinds of help available, the young alcoholic can be spared
years of misery, both for himself and everybody else around him.
It may be possible to arrest the illness *before* he takes on the
responsibilities of a family, and this must be better than starting
a family before the illness has shown itself.

One of the difficulties concerning young alcoholics is the fact
that, because of their ages, they cannot imagine that they can
possibly be alcoholics. They have in their mind a picture of what
an alcoholic should look like, and because it in no way measures
up to what they themselves are, they see no connection between
this image and themselves. They see the alcoholic as a pathetic
old tramp, huddled in a shop doorway, wrapped in papers and
drinking a brand of the cheapest plonk. If he deteriorates from
that position, then he is lying on the embankment drinking meths,
or worse still shivering on some derelict site along with the other
down-and-outs.

Strenuous Denial

The young problem drinker would strenuously deny (and rightly)
that he is in any way allied to those pathetic people. He could
state that he has a nice home, or that he still has a decent job.
He could say that he only drinks beer, or that he only drinks at
night time in the local. The fact that he doesn't feel too bad and
that there are no 'shakes' to worry him in the morning also paints
a picture that all is under control. Again, it must be stressed that
it is not so much *what* one drinks, or *where* or *when*, but *how*
it affects one that determines whether one has a problem or not.

If a young person *needs* booze to enable him or her to do
anything, then they have a problem. They may not be allied to
the pathetic old tramp — yet. But if they are alcoholics and they

go on drinking alcohol, anything goes. And eventually *everything* goes.

But the young alcoholic doesn't have to sink to the depths that some of his older brothers and sisters have sunk to. They don't have to experience the 'drying out' clinics, or the long spells in the special units. They don't have to suffer the indignities of gaol sentences, or know the mental anguish of 'locked wards' in hospitals.

A bit hard, you think? Not if it prevents *one* young person from going through the horrors that await the alcoholic who decides to carry on drinking alcohol.

So, if a youngster finds that he can't remember just what happened last night at the party or whatever, he is suffering from blackouts, and is on the start of a very slippery slope. If he 'only comes alive' after a drink — he must watch it. There are plenty of danger signals around, but the most potent question of all is: Can I take it *or* leave it? If the honest answer is 'If I take it *I can't* leave it,' then he has a problem. And he, too, can be helped.

6.

THE FAMILY ILLNESS

The effects of alcoholism spread throughout a family with the same disastrous consequences as a prairie fire. They may not have the same speed as a fire, but the results are just as devastating. And whether it is the father or the mother who is the practising alcoholic, the effects of their drinking cannot be anything else but a bewildering heartache for all those who have to put up with it. Many, of course, do not put up with it and leave at the first opportunity. Children of drinking alcoholics have invariably seen a home life that has steadily deteriorated over the years, and they make a firm avowal that at a certain age they will be out of it all. This in itself causes heartache, for it may mean leaving a well-loved mother to cope with a drunken father; or it could mean leaving a father who has struggled for years to bring up the family to get on with the job of coping with a drunken wife.

The Family Suffers
There is no easy way out. If there is a drinking alcoholic in the family, then someone as well as the drinker is going to suffer. Children, in the main, are the real innocent sufferers of the alcoholic parent. The love that should be theirs by right is too often denied them; or, if it is given, it is given in such a manner that it just cannot be understood by the children.

The spouses of drinking alcoholics have at least some recourse to action, especially when they are at their wits' end as to what to do. They can argue with the partner about the drinking habits and what they are doing to the family. They can reason with him (or her) to try and see just what a state the family is getting into or is already in. They can even try drinking with the partner in the hope that they can turn what is now a 'loner's suicide trail' into a social habit that will in some way lessen the problem that is now apparent to all concerned. They can find the bottles that are either on show in the cabinet or hidden all over the house, and pour booze down the sink. They can ask for help from the family doctor, or priest, and they can even, in a fit of sheer exasperation, walk out of the house. But, if there are children involved, they will invariably come back, hoping that their show of 'strength' must in some way have had an effect that will bring the drinker to his senses.

The chances of any of these methods being successful as far as the drinking alcoholic is concerned are, regretfully, remote. There can be no doubt that the screams of a wife about her husband's drinking, and the abuse hurled at him for the damage he is causing to her and the family, does not entirely fall on deaf ears. The man *knows* that what she says is true. He is aware that, as a father to his children, his performance is less than expected. He *knows* that as a husband, lover and provider, he leaves much to be desired; and wherever he looks he sees the creaking structure of a family life that was, perhaps, at one time a happy and close-knit unit.

A Feeling of Failure

He sometimes admits quite freely that it is his fault and that he will do something about it; but every attempt at a remedy usually meets with failure, and each feeling of failure usually brings a burning desire to escape back to the world where there are no screaming wives, no abuse, no sobbing children and no scorn at his attempts to be the man he once was — and we know how to 'escape' back into that little world. The nearest bottle provides an instant passport to the land of make-believe; and the fact that the 'cost' of a trip has now increased somewhat is not lost upon those who are left in the world of stark reality.

But if the wife of the drinking alcoholic can, however ineffectively, drink with, scream at or walk out on and come back to the husband, there is little or nothing that the children can do, especially if they are young. They can but observe a home life that is as different from their friends' as it is possible to be. They can feel the resentment, rage and hopelessness of the mother, and they can feel the resentment, rage and hopelessness of the father. It is a baffling, complex and frightening experience, and their world is indeed an unenviable one that has more than its fair share of tears.

Inconsistent Relationship

Probably the most baffling aspect of the child's life with the alcoholic father is the sheer inconsistency of the relationship. The father can be the most loving of parents at times. He can laugh with the family, take an interest in their welfare and be everything that is desired of him. And then, in the space of but an hour, he can change from the loving father into an inconsiderate, selfish and don't-give-a-damn drinker.

The loving and caring part of his nature is usually shown when he is not drinking, or has just had sufficient to put him into that particular mood. But once he has had one drink over his particular borderline — goodbye, Doctor Jekyll; hello, Mister Hyde. The fact that the children are never quite sure just who they are going to get each day (Mister Hyde does appear with more regularity as the illness progresses) makes for an uneasy life, to say the least; and it is not to be wondered at that there is a grim determination to get away from it all at the first opportunity.

Unless there is some form of secure income, sooner or later the wife of the drinking alcoholic will also have financial difficulties. She will, all things being equal, try to cope with them. As the husband drinks more and more, it will be left to her to see to it that the family is provided for, both in welfare and love. She will assume (she has to) the role of both father and mother, and she invariably develops a 'strength' that comes with the fulfilling of a dual role. It is a fact that the father can at times be totally ignored in the home, and the wife will settle for whatever money he does provide. It is not unknown for them to have separate beds, or even rooms, for by this time the husband may simply want to be left alone to get on with his drinking and to be spared the rows and rages and the children's hostility in a disunited family.

Violence

One of the most distressing aspects in a family where it is the father who is drinking is the common occurrence of violence. It may be he is by his very nature a violent man, and it is the alcohol that brings this violence to the fore. But it is also possible that he is not violent and it is only when he drinks alcohol that he becomes vicious. So both wife and children may go in absolute fear and terror of just who will arrive home, or wake up, when the alcoholic father is drinking.

The Remorse of the Alcoholic

Also heart-rending is the remorse of the alcoholic when he realizes what he has done to the wife and children who he may love so very dearly. He begs for forgiveness and swears on all that is holy that it will never happen again. He cannot understand how he could possibly have hurt in any way a family who mean so much to him, and his regrets are as real as were his attacks.

This type can try to make up to the family with excessive gifts, flowers, toys, and all the other offerings of the penitent alcoholic. And while this may work in the early stages, it is not very long before the wife and family refuse to fall for this type of gift-offering.

They only want one thing: for Dad to stop drinking. And this he seems unable to do. And so the sad saga continues . . . drink, sorrow, remorse, drink, guilt, anger, drink, promises, gifts, drinking . . . . The list is endless and the merry-go-round seems never-ending.

When the Mother is an Alcoholic

But the fear and bewilderment that the family of an alcoholic father experience when Dad is 'at it' is even worse when it is Mum who is 'at it'. Here is a situation that nature did not intend to happen. As was stated previously, although the drunken man may be either accepted or tolerated, the drunken woman is neither accepted nor tolerated. And because of this situation, a woman alcoholic, especially when the illness is beginning to bite deep, is usually a lonely, sad, frightened and secret drinker.

The first sign that all is not well is the fact that the pride in the home, which may well have been a strong point in the past, is now no longer important. She may try in the early stages to pretend that everything is all right, and so the housework, shopping, meals, etc. will be seen to. But if the woman alcoholic *keeps* on drinking, there is nothing on God's earth that can stop the rot from eventually showing itself in the home. The housework will *not* be completed; the shopping will *not* be done — and if it is, more bottles than anything else will be bought. The meals will lose the care that was formerly lavished upon them, and the whole place will, sooner or later, show only too well that the 'woman's touch' is no longer there. Father and children are indeed sorry cases when Mum is slowly changing before their eyes from the woman she was to the woman she now is. The deterioration is more obvious because she is, by the very nature of her position, at home, and the change is there for all to see.

Her drinking will probably start when both husband and

children are away at work and school respectively. Tremendous efforts are made to 'pull herself together' before they all get home, and in the early days this is accomplished without too much notice being paid. But notice *will* be paid no matter how much she tries to hide the fact, and eventually the rows and the criticisms will start.

Criticism Does Not Help

The sad fact about rows and criticisms is that no matter how justified they may be, they are of no help to the practising alcoholic. The rows, criticisms, hostility and condemnations are four of the main factors in the making of the secret drinker. If an alcoholic, whether male or female, was answerable to no one, and knew that no matter what he did or said there would be no repercussions, then the chances are that he would just drink away, not giving a damn for anyone. But when an alcoholic *does* have responsibilities, and does care for others, then he invariably makes promises about his drinking, usually to the effect that he will either 'cool it' or quit entirely.

Secret Drinking

When an alcoholic makes promises of this nature and then finds himself incapable of keeping them, it is not unusual for him to turn to secret drinking. After all, how on earth can a person make a solemn vow never to touch the stuff again and then pour and drink a glass of booze? And once a promise not to drink again has been made and been broken, this brings the pangs of guilt, remorse and resentment that are well known to the alcoholic drinker.

Promises not to drink again are usually made with absolute sincerity by the alcoholic, and these promises are — at least in the beginning — accepted by the family with sheer relief and heartfelt thanks. But when the desire for a drink comes, it is not only the physical craving that besets the drinker but also the mental obsession; and when those two get to work, the odds against the alcoholic taking the first drink are indeed short. The fact that a promise not to drink has been broken must invariably lead to lies and 'cover-ups', for in answer to the question, 'Have you been drinking?', the answer is invariably, 'Certainly not.'

It is when the accusations and denials start that the drinker usually tries to hide the fact that he has been drinking, and many methods have been used (with, at first, some success) to cover it up. The first thing he does (apart from strenuously denying the fact that he has had a drink in the first place) is to try and hide the smell of booze. That is why vodka is a favourite tipple with alcoholics: they think that the smell of it is not noticeable. There are also many aids to help drinkers in the quest for a 'non-showable' drink.

They use mouth sprays, eat pickled onions, nibble bits of cheese — there are another dozen tried and trusted methods. It doesn't seem to strike them (or the writer when he did the same thing) that all the spouse has to do is observe the now obvious subtle personality change, listen for the strenuous and vehement denials that no drink has passed their lips, and smell the unmistakable odour of TCP or some similar antiseptic. These factors in themselves are not a hundred per cent indication that the alcoholic is again drinking — but you can usually lay odds on it!

An Accomplished Liar

The other snag about making promises never to touch another drop is that you are expected to keep your promise. So, when the promiser finds that he/she *needs* a drink, and *must* have one, the chances are that there is no booze handy. The family, fully expecting that the promises will be adhered to, may well have got rid of the stuff, and probably avowed that never again will any booze be allowed in the house. So, when an alcoholic needs a drink, say, at 7 a.m., some excuse must be made to leave whatever room he happens to be in; and if he makes for the garage — then there must be a supply of drink there. Once he takes a drink he is left with the problem of 'covering up', and back we go on the 'Have you?', 'No, I haven't' performance. The practising alcoholic, when drinking within the family unit, by the very nature of things *must* be an accomplished liar. However, as time goes on, he does not even try to cover up. He knows that no one believes him, whatever he says; and besides, what is the use of drinking vodka, nibbling cheese and pickled onions, denying strenuously that he has had a drink — and then falling over the door mat? Whatever way one decides to try and hide the fact that one has had a drink, alcohol itself will give it away. All one has to do is observe and listen.

There comes a time when, if an alcoholic takes a drink, there is just no way of hiding the fact. The stuff speaks for itself.

As we have seen, a practising alcoholic in a family goes hand in hand with rows and recriminations. It is impossible to have a drinking spouse and an absence of acrimony. 'Look what you are doing to us' is an all too familiar accusation hurled at the drinker; and as the drinker hears the accusation he or she either ignores it completely, or tries to make counter-accusations. He can slam the door and make for the nearest pub, off-licence, or hidden bottle, or can yet again make the promise to 'pull myself together'.

But the alcoholic who is drinking under these conditions is, sooner or later, beset by feelings of both guilt and remorse. And for good measure you can also throw in self-pity. The three are impossible to disassociate from the alcoholic drinker, for what was once a pleasurable hobby is now a very painful (or will be) occupation.

There must be guilt for, no matter how they try to dodge the issue, they *know* deep within themselves that it is *their* behaviour that is causing the upset in the family. There are, of course, exceptions, and a great many alcoholics have seen their family life destroyed beyond repair and still considered that their drinking either had nothing to do with it, or that somehow or another the family should have understood their drinking.

Self-pity

As for self-pity, alcoholism was weaned upon the most fundamental of characteristics. 'Poor me' is part of the drinker's everyday vocabulary. 'Why me?' is another phrase that cannot be left out, and 'they don't understand' is another that comes high on the list of the tippler's phrase book. The hard facts of the matter are that the more the alcoholic sinks into a state of self-pity, the more he sees himself as a victim of some conspiracy; a conspiracy that has somehow turned him into a moral weakling, social outcast, and hard-done-by character.

It is almost impossible for the drinking alcoholic to contemplate a day of not drinking, without first having a drink while contemplating it! And so it will be seen that the phrase 'I'll just have one to pull myself together' is another *must* for the alcoholic's book. The fact that the 'one' is the lighting of the fuse is lost upon him, and the length of the fuse is anyone's guess. But once the fuse is lit, the explosion is inevitable. And so we have the sorry state of the once-loving husband or wife visibly changing before the family's eyes. The fact that they make such strenuous efforts to hide the problem goes in some way to show that they don't really want this state of affairs. They want to drink like they once did. They want the love, companionship and friendship that in the past came from the family (or should have done), but it is now coming from the bottle. And as was stated previously, the moment that alcohol is taken for any reason other than social . . . expect trouble.

But can the alcoholic regain the love, companionship and friendship of family and others? Is it possible that the sad and sorrowful state that is now obvious to all (including the drinker) can be overcome? Can there be some form of recovery whereby he is once again the loved and respected person he once was? You had better believe it — the answer is most definitely Yes.

7.

HOW CAN I TELL IF I'M AN ALCOHOLIC?

'How can I tell if I'm an alcoholic?' is a question that has been asked by countless millions of good folk, and many of them are really and truly seeking an answer. But, in a great many cases, a verbal answer is not sufficient — they need more practical proof, and there are several ways in which persons who *think* that they may be alcoholics can put the question to the acid test. This is to their good, for it will show them (whether they accept the findings or not is another matter) just what their position is *vis-à-vis* booze.

It has been said that the operative word when discussing the alcoholic is *control*, and the tests or experiments to determine whether that control is still there or not can be an enlightening and pleasant experience — or it can be an enlightening and disastrous fiasco.

Has the Control Gone?
There are many ways in which the 'Am I, or am I not?' drinker can determine whether the control has gone or not, and they all, of course, involve the taking of alcohol. One such test concerns the phrase 'No more for me, I've had enough'. The phrase has been used in bars, restaurants, clubs and social gatherings of all kinds since men and women first got together on licensed premises, or, as the case may be, unlicensed premises. But it is a phrase that is unknown to the practising alcoholic. So, here is our yardstick: we will use the phrase 'I've had enough' after a certain agreed amount of booze has been drunk. To be effective, this experiment must be carried out over a certain length of time; let us say, in this instance, a period of six months.

Firstly, the person concerned in the experiment will decide to take a certain amount of his favourite tipple *every other day*, and that he will take *no more and no less* than the agreed amount. If, for example, he was drinking vodka, then an amount of, say, four large ones on his 'on' days will be enough to allow him to have a drink at lunchtime (this being considered as normal drinking time) should he so desire. He may, of course, like to have a couple in his local after a day's work; so, if he has two at lunchtime, he still has two left for his evening drink. If he fancies one at home to finish the day off, he can so ration himself that he allows for this. Four large ones can be said to be sufficient to see a 'social' drinker through all contingencies; and if he *is* a social drinker, and does not *need* alcohol to function, this should enable him to have the best of both worlds.

The reason for having his social drinking every *other* day is to show that, on waking up after his 'on' days, he can, whether the desire to drink is there or not, say with complete conviction and authority: 'Not today, thank you!'

If a drinker can accept these conditions and can carry them out to the letter, although it may not be *absolute* proof that he is not an alcoholic, it is a hundred to one against him being one. And the reason is that once an alcoholic has taken alcohol, and this becomes more apparent as the illness progresses, he is in no position to give guarantees as to his subsequent drinking pattern.

The 'No More' Rule

Another test of control is to agree to someone else saying 'You've had enough.' Can there be anything more difficult for the alcoholic to agree to than being told 'No more' just when he is getting the taste? So, again, we agree on a plan. At some time during the experiment — and it could be in the local, or at a party, or merely at home — someone, usually the spouse, will ask the drinker to refrain from having any more booze. This request usually comes when the spouse, or whoever, can see the subtle personality change taking place as the alcohol starts to take effect. Now, if under these conditions a drinker can agree to accept the 'no more' rule, and keep this up for the six months' period, then again the chances are he is not an alcoholic.

Failing the Tests

But what if, on accepting these conditions, our drinker fails to carry them out? What if he advances reasons (and they are usually good reasons) as to why he should make an exception on one of his 'off booze' days and turn it into an 'on booze' day? And what if, just as he is beginning to feel the old glow taking effect, someone says 'That's enough', and he is expected to let that glow last him through the rest of the evening without adding to it by the use of more booze?

If he makes excuses as to why he should carry on, or even try intellectual arguments as to why the experiment was silly in the first place, or maybe absolutely refuses to have anything to do with the experiment (this refusal comes once he has heard the dreaded words 'No more'), our drinking friend may have to face the possibility that the control he thought he had just isn't there any more. These two experiments are fraught with danger as they may involve an alcoholic in drinking alcohol to try to prove the fact that he isn't one. But when an alcoholic takes alcohol, there is invariably trouble for someone, and all he usually proves is the fact that his need for booze is now even more out of control than it was previously. But there are times when a problem drinker needs *convincing,* and if these experiments can do that, then they may well be worth the risk.

Many drinkers have arrived at the conclusion that they are in fact alcoholics without having to sink to the depths to prove the fact. There are a great number of people who became aware that their lives were becoming unmanageable through drinking too much or, even if they didn't drink too much, that what they did drink caused trouble; and at a certain stage in their drinking they said 'enough'. It is obvious to them that the way in which they were drinking, quite apart from the amount of booze consumed, was in no way normal; and the pleas from the family, friends and colleagues alike were taken to heart before any great damage was done. Such alcoholics are the lucky ones.

The alcoholic who wants to get off the stuff, and who can get over the first initial period of physical craving, knows that if he sticks it out, the craving will go and he will be free, in much the same way as the smoker who gets over the first few weeks without a smoke will also be free of the habit.

The Mental Obsession
If the desire is strong enough to *stay* free, then the chances are that the former smoker need never go back to his cigarettes again. The same *could* be said for the drinker who has the desire to remain free of alcohol, but in his case there is another factor at work; a much more powerful and subtle factor, and one that is as baffling and complex as any condition known

to man — the Mental Obsession.

It is not all that difficult to accept the conclusion that if a person drinks alcohol (or takes any other drug), there is a possibility that he will become addicted to that particular drug. This is known as Physical Addiction and can indeed be a distressing condition. Patients in hospital who have to be given 'hard' drugs such as morphine as a pain reliever have the drug administered strictly in accordance with medical advice and supervision, otherwise it is possible that the patient could become addicted to the drug, and that this addiction could become a much worse condition than the original complaint.

But what strange factor makes a person who knows that alcohol is harmful to him, after a certain length of time off the stuff, pick up the first drink which will in turn lead to the first bottle, and so on? Why is it that a seemingly intelligent individual, who has a family, a nice home, a good job and all the other things that are commonly associated with the 'normal' adult, will pick up a glass of booze that he knows will probably cost him all the aforementioned things? What strange reasoning takes place that will compel a person to do the one thing he should *not* do? Is there logic in his reasoning that the thing which has defeated him so many times in the past is now under his control, even when it can be proved beyond doubt that millions of others have failed in the same, strange, hopeless and pathetic quest?

If reason, intelligence and sheer logic were to rise to the fore in this situation, no alcoholic who has suffered from the illness of alcoholism would ever again pour the stuff down his throat. But the fact that reasonable, intelligent and logical people who are alcoholics do pour the stuff down their throats proves that there is a factor at work here that needs more comment than that the person concerned is a moral weakling and social misfit.

Physical addiction can be broken, and there are thousands of people walking around today who can attest to this fact. If a person cannot break the habit of drinking alcohol, then it may be that they will have to be kept forcibly from the stuff. Put a person who is drinking himself to death in gaol and the physical addiction will soon be arrested. Put him in hospital where it is impossible for him to have access to alcohol, and it will not be long before the physical craving goes, along with the shakes, sweats and the rest of the alcoholic's symptoms. But experience shows that when the alcoholic comes out from his enforced stay in gaol or hospital, if the mental side of the illness hasn't been treated in some way or another it is only a matter of time before he will commence his drinking habits, only this time with greater intensity than before.

Why Start Again?

Ask almost any alcoholic who has started drinking again after a spell off the stuff just why he did it, and the chances are that there will be no definite answer that makes any sense.

There is, of course, one answer that does make sense, and that is 'Because I just fancied drinking again.' That, at least, would be honest. But that answer is seldom if ever given in answer to the question.

One usually gets 'I'm not too sure', or 'I don't know why I did it', and 'This time I thought I could handle the stuff' is a favourite one.

An Uphill Battle

And so the mental obsession drives him towards the first drink, which in turn creates a physical compulsion. And between the physical compulsion and the mental obsession, the alcoholic is indeed fighting an uphill battle. Many, many people have fought the battle against booze on the physical compulsion field and have managed to stay sober. But it is a hard battle and they are always in danger of taking that first drink. The subtle forces of the mental side lie in wait for the unwary, and should they drop their guard for a second, it strikes. It may be a feeling of great elation, or a feeling of great depression; it could be when they are feeling at their best in company, or at their worst all alone. Lower the guard of awareness and the enemy will strike. It will come in the guise of a friend, an old pal, a comforter, a strength, or even as an escape route from present difficulties, or sheer boredom.

But whatever guise it comes in, it is still the great 'con' artiste. The legions of alcoholics who have fallen victim to its wiles are legendary. So, you will see that the alcoholic who has stopped drinking and who wants to stay stopped, must not only see the illness of alcoholism as a physical one, but also as a mental one.

The alcoholic indeed has not only a *drinking* problem but also a *thinking* problem. Tackling one and not the other invites trouble. So now we know how our 'enemy' operates. He doesn't fight fair. But what enemy ever did, especially when the stakes are so high. And can there be any higher stakes than one's own life? There are many methods of dealing with the *thinking* problem of the alcoholic, and they are discussed in the following chapters. But without doubt one of the biggest mistakes that an alcoholic can make is to think that merely to stop drinking alcohol will solve the problem. The alcoholic who merely stops drinking leaves a big void; a void that in the past has been filled with alcohol. That void *must* be replaced with something else. But what? Is there anything that can replace booze? And will the replacement be an adequately potent substitute for that which did so much for the drinker in days gone by? The answer is Yes.

8.

HOW TO STOP

The alcoholic may well have had some success with both his 'controlled' drinking attempts and also his 'never again' assertions. But, of course, the only way controlled drinking can be deemed effective is for that control to be exercised over a very long time.

To say that one will only have half a bottle of wine each night with a meal is indeed controlled drinking — providing it is kept up for, say, a number of years. But to keep it up for a month and then to slip into the state where the 'odd' brandy is taken with the coffee is to lose, however slowly, that control.

If an alcoholic keeps on drinking, there will come a time when he simply *cannot* stop, and either he or his family will have to take measures to prevent him from drinking himself to death. There are various methods of help available, and some of them include actual treatment for the illness of alcoholism — an illness which the sufferer, even at this stage of the game, may still not accept that he has. It may seem a contradiction in terms to say that he can know deep down in his heart that the control has gone and yet refuse to accept the fact. Again, it must be stated that this illness is one of the most baffling and complex conditions known to man. What can be so obvious to everyone else seems to be lost upon the drinker. The problem here is that the alcoholic does not want to admit the truth, so he allows the delusory part of the illness to have a field day; and he keeps looking, even up to the gates of the cemetery itself, for a way to drink without the consequences. But assuming that he, or someone, forces the issue, here are some of the methods of treatment that can offer hope to the drinking alcoholic.

Family Doctor
A visit to the family doctor is usually the first move made by the

person who thinks he may have a drinking problem. This is not a bad thing. Anything that brings out into the open the fact that booze is beginning to cause problems must be beneficial to the person concerned.

The doctor may attempt to treat his patient as best he can; and there is no doubt that, providing the doctor has been told the whole truth about the drinking habits of the patient, some relief can be obtained. For a start there will be a physical examination, and this may reveal that certain physical damage has been done. The fact that this damage is being treated is usually a relief to the patient, and he sometimes thinks himself lucky that the damage is as slight as it is. This may well bring about an attitude of 'I'll quit drinking before things get any worse', and if that does happen, the person concerned is indeed fortunate.

Again, the doctor may only find that his patient is lacking in certain vitamins, and a course of pills plus a stern warning to 'get hold of yourself' may do the trick. Again, if this 'treatment' brings about a change in the patient, all well and good.

The doctor, if he recognizes that he is dealing with a practising alcoholic, may admit straightaway that he is not qualified to deal with this particular illness and suggest some other form of available treatment. This is a refreshing attitude, for in the family doctor admitting that alcoholism is a mite outside the scope of the normal G.P. lies the patient's best hope of specialized treatment and eventual recovery.

The main snag in a family doctor dealing with alcoholism is the fact that he seldom gets the *truth* about the patient's drinking habits. It is not the doctor's fault, nor is it the patient's. The fact that he *is* suffering from alcoholism precludes him from being honest about it all. The alcoholic seldom seeks help in the first instance to stop him drinking. The great majority of them just cannot envisage life without alcohol, and they seek a form of help that will enable them either to cut down on their drinking (control), or else a method whereby they can drink without the consequences of their drinking, and as we have seen, no one has yet found a way to achieve these objectives.

Hospital Treatment

This is, at best, a temporary measure. Very few hospitals have either the staff or facilities to deal with the drinking alcoholic — or, as they may term him or her, the drunk. If a person is carried into hospital suffering from the effects of alcohol, he is (provided the space is available) placed into a 'drying out' ward for a few days. He may be given vitamin injections or tablets, as it will be obvious to the doctors that he is deficient in these vitamins. If he is fortunate, he may see the hospital psychiatrist, and this may well bring home to him the seriousness of his position. The fact that he is having 'enforced sobriety' will, providing he is kept there long enough, get rid of the 'shakes' that he has very likely been experiencing. And this, coupled with the fact that he is also having some decent nights' sleep (with, perhaps, the aid of sleeping tablets) will usually have a tremendous effect on him. It is likely that once he starts to feel better he will assure doctors, nurses, psychiatrists and family alike that he has learned his lesson and that his drinking days are over.

The promises and assertions are in themselves not lies; they are made with as much sincerity as the alcoholic can muster. But the promises that are made in the confines of a nice, clean room, where there is, perhaps, a fair amount of attention and consideration, are a lot harder to keep once that room and attention are no more. Once the pressures of the 'outside world' return, the chances are that the temporary relief of the hospital will soon be forgotten. This is not the fault of the hospitals. They are limited both in facilities and knowledge for the treatment of the world's third biggest killer illness, alcoholism.

There must be other and more successful methods of treatment, and there are.

Hypnosis

The idea here is that the thought to drink alcohol is supplanted by the thought *not* to drink alcohol. In some way or another the drinker must be convinced that booze is unattractive. This method of treatment has had some, very limited, success. The real problem here is that the hypnotist is, in the main, trying to implant a thought into the patient's mind that the patient doesn't believe anyway. The hypnotist is trying to get through to the drinker that booze is bad for him — and here is the snag. For the drinker does not believe that booze is bad for him. What is bad for him is his inability to control the stuff. So, at a very deep level of consciousness, the patient has a conflict going on. The hypnotist is trying to instil a positive thought into him that he — the patient — rejects. The hypnotist may suggest that every time the drinker takes alcohol it will taste awful. It is not unknown for a practising alcoholic to find the taste of a drink awful. In the

latter stages of the illness every drink tastes awful! If taste were
to be the criterion then an alcoholic who is nearing the end of
the line would never have another drink. At this stage, alcohol
merely makes him sick and ill. But taste is not what the alcoholic
is concerned about. It is effect he is after.

It may be that the hypnotist will try and suggest that the drinker
has no need of the effect of alcohol, and that he can live quite
well without the euphoric spell cast by it. One cannot argue with
the logic of that reasoning, but if an alcoholic has become
dependent on the stuff not only for the alleviation of the physical
craving but also for the alleviation of the mental obsession, the
hypnotist must be able to offer something that will replace the
magic spell cast by our old master illusionist, alcohol.

Has the hypnotist any such alternative? A few say 'Yes', and good
luck to them. But when one thinks of the numbers who suffer
from alcoholism, and then think of the number of competent
hypnotists who are able to understand the magnitude of their
task, it becomes clear that this is at best a solution for the limited
few.

Religion
The practising alcoholic has probably offered more prayers to
whatever god he adheres to than any other person on this earth.
The reason for that is because, as the illness progresses, he suffers
more than most people on this earth. He knows physical pain
and he experiences mental anguish. The chances are that his job
is in jeopardy, as is his family life. His wife rages, screams, cries,
criticizes, condemns, and blames. His children are alienated to
a point whereby he is virtually alone. His friends drop off one
by one as his drinking 'nears the end' and if, as is usually the case,
he has tried to avert the apparent disaster by having hospital, clinic
or psychiatric treatment, etc., he sees no way out of his problem
other than a miracle. From time immemorial, those seeking
miracles have turned to the unknown source: God.

Again it must be said that there have been cases where chronic
alcoholics have, in desperation, appealed to their 'highest ultimate
authority' for help, and the seemingly impossible has happened:
the obsession to drink has disappeared. But these cases are
conspicuous by their infrequency. There are few sadder sights
than the suffering alcoholic appealing to the unknown god for
help and hearing nothing in reply, except maybe the clink of
another bottle. Priests will pray with him and for him. And

eventually, when he has made the most solemn promises and signed every pledge in the book, even the priest will have to shake his head in despair and bewilderment at the drinker's inability — even with the asked-for divine help — to resolve this problem.

They cannot understand (as even the drinker cannot understand) why it is that a man or woman who may have been a strong member of the Church, and who has shown strength and fortitude in other ways, can be so unable to behave like a rational member of society when it comes to drinking alcohol. They promise to abstain and fail. They ask forgiveness, then lie about their drinking. They ask forgiveness for their lies, then drink again. Was there ever a more distressing situation? The priests try to understand, and it is to their credit that the drinker is seldom if ever refused what help they can give. But by the very nature of things, that help is limited. If understanding and compassion were a cure for alcoholism, then religion would have the answer to one of the world's greatest problems.

But, unfortunately, understanding and compassion are not enough. They are welcome indeed to those who are suffering from alcoholism, but something of a much deeper nature is needed.

It is interesting to note that the Pope issued a decree recently whereby priests who are alcoholics are excused from drinking fermented communion wine. The reason for this is because the number of priests who are alcoholics is growing, and it is causing a serious problem in the Church. Probably the saddest aspect of the alcoholic priest is that fact that often it is the communion wine that is drunk to satisfy his craving. The fact that it is consecrated is neither here nor there — especially once the first drink has gone down.

Specialized Clinic Treatment

When a person who is well-known in the public eye states quite openly that he or she is an alcoholic, this surely can be deemed as a most courageous act. There are, in fact, many famous people who have made this assertion — footballers, boxers, entertainers, film stars, politicians and astronauts among them. Without doubt, however, when the famous person happens to be the wife of the American President, it makes her declaration all the more remarkable.

Betty Ford, America's former First Lady decided to declare not only her alcoholic suffering but also her subsequent and continuing recovery, and the reason for her decision was quite simple: 'If my admission can encourage the suffering alcoholic to seek the specialized help they so desperately need — remember, alcoholism is an illness, not a weakness — then my admission will not have been made in vain.'

There are thousands of people alive today who owe their lives to Betty Ford's decision to 'go public' and the fact that she had the full support of her husband says much for his courage also.

Betty Ford was so grateful for all the help she received from so many sources — especially the clinic she attended for her problem — she decided to lend her name to such a clinic in Palm Springs, California and many of the best-known names in show business have had treatment for alcohol or drug addiction there. But the clinic is not only for the famous: a 'John Doe' is as welcome there as was Robert Mitchum; 'Mary Smith' is as welcome as was Elizabeth Taylor. There are many Betty Ford-type clinics in operation now, and to this lady must go much of the credit for their proliferation.

Specialized clinic treatment is run in much the same way as that of specialized hospital treatment, but the treatment is much more comprehensive than that of the hospital.

Many clinics, of course, do take some National Health patients as well as those with private health insurance, and the stay is normally that of one to three months. But if anyone thinks that the cost of a particular clinic is somewhat excessive, let them reflect on the cost if they continued to drink. Seen in that light, whatever the clinic's cost, it is cheap at half the price if alcoholics stop drinking. And they do!

Clinics have their own medical staff in attendance, and, on admission, the new patient is given a complete medical. If suffering physically (shakes, etc.) they will receive all the necessary medication to alleviate their condition.

Many patients have tried to smuggle either alcohol or pills (or both) into the clinic with them, but the staff — many of them recovering alcoholics — are wise to every trick in the trade. They really are experts in the art of 'kidology', and the new arrival is soon very much aware of the fact.

Although they are paying for their stay, the patients are in no way treated as though they are in a holiday camp. This is not a health farm where their every whim is attended to. They are not there for the treatment of some superficial ailment, they are there for the treatment of alcoholism and there is no easy road for them to meander down at their leisure.

The question could be asked: Why didn't all those people just pop into the nearest meeting of Alcoholics Anonymous instead of getting themselves involved in a lengthy and fairly expensive stay at a private clinic?

The answers are, in the main, threefold:

1. They simply could not bring themselves to walk into a room full of strangers; after all, 'someone might see them.'
2. They had already tried AA and found that it just wasn't for them.
3. As a well-known 'personality', they would stand out like the proverbial sore thumb at an AA meeting.
    All valid and acceptable answers. So, whatever the reason for preferring a private clinic to that of any other type of treatment, the fact that so many people have benefitted from them justifies their existence.

Although alcoholics are all in the same boat during their stay at the clinic, they are also in the same room, it being quite normal that they are required to share with someone of the same sex. They also have to clean the room and do their own washing, ironing and so on. Many of the clinics require the patients to do the cooking and the washing up and this, in itself, is a great leveller. Often for the first time in years they are being asked to accept a life-style that insists upon their 'sharing', and it has been found that nothing but good can come from such an experience. Many patients, at the start of the course, object to this regime, but it is that or nothing. There are no 'stars' at such clinics, and if they don't like it they are free to leave anytime they want to. That so few do so says much for the psychology of the system. When a West End star is washing the dishes, and a suburban housewife is drying them, both learn something from the experience that could not possibly be learned by any other method.

New patients will be gradually introduced into the group therapy meetings and there, under the guidance of a very experienced counsellor, they will be coaxed (gently and, at times, not so gently) into 'coming clean' about their previous life-style.

As it is absolutely impossible for an alcoholic to mature as a person whilst he or she is drinking, the chances are that, when the patient eventually does start to 'open up', it will be a total mixture of truths, half-truths, illusion and delusion — a mixture well known to counsellors and recovering alcoholics everywhere. The things that they say will be said in the total belief that what they are saying is really true, and it is only as the sessions continue and the patient is reminded, either by their counsellor or another member of the group, just what they did say a few days previously, that they will slowly begin to realize just what a mess their life has been in.

And if *their* life has been in a mess, there is also another unit that has been in as big a mess — that of the family of the patient. There is no way that anyone close to a drinking alcoholic can escape the mayhem created by this condition.

Stopping drinking is but the first step on the long road to recovery, but it is the most important step of all. Without it, no recovery is possible. It must be said that when an alcoholic does stop drinking, it can be a frightening experience; for the first time in years they will see life as it really is and be faced with the reality of their situation. But there is one thing for sure: it can only get better. When the spotlight of awareness is beamed upon a subject, that subject however painful to behold, can not only be seen but can also be dealt with.

There will be many other aspects of their stay at the clinic that will be an absolute revelation to the now rapidly 'sobering-up' patients, and one of the most popular is the regular video shows. These are given by some of the most experienced speakers in the field of alcoholism recovery and the fact that they are given with not only total sincerity, based upon empiric experience, but also given with a sense of humour makes all the difference between audience acceptance and audience rejection. There are times when it takes one not only to know one but also to get through to one.

When a talk on such a serious subject as alcoholism — it is the third of the world's 'killer' conditions — is given in such a manner, it portrays to the patient that it is indeed possible to live a happy, normal life without booze. There is nothing funny about the suffering alcoholic but, conversely, there is something marvellous about the recovering one. And laughter is a necessary part of that recovery.

Why Alcoholics Drink

'You only drank to steady your nerves, their steadiness to improve, last night you got so steady, you couldn't even move.'

Substitute the following for the word 'Nerves' and you have to hand the answers given by alcoholics as to why they drink:

Insomnia, Pressure of work, No work, Hyperactive, Lethargic, Happy, Unhappy, Wife/Husband left me, Wife/Husband came back, the list goes on. It should be remembered by all those who try to help alcoholics to recover that, when alcoholics drink, they drink not so much because they want to, but *because they have to.* Alcoholics drink because they are addicted and all the other reasons are by-products of this problem.

It is no coincidence that, once an alcoholic has stopped drinking, stays stopped, and has taken certain steps to mature as a normal adult, all the other problems seem to sort themselves out.

When discussing the merits of special clinics and those of AA, it can truly be said that whilst the former *gets* you sober, the latter *keeps* you sober. A winning pair! It is to the credit of such clinics that they realize the importance of AA and make attendance at their meetings a 'must'.

Meetings are held at the clinic and the patients are also taken to the local meetings of AA at the nearest town. Many patients object to their mandatory attendance at such meetings and take the attitude, 'Why should I have to go to AA here? I could have gone to the meetings without coming to a clinic and have it pushed down my throat.' Maybe they would.

AA is a bit like flu: it's infectious. To see people weekly, however reluctantly, sharing their sobriety in a matter that is impossible not to admire, plants the seed of 'I Want What They Have'. It may take a long time for that seed to bear fruit, but in the majority of cases it works.

Eventually patients see that AA is not being 'pushed down their throats'. They will be told that the moment they leave the clinic, if they want to drink, so be it. They can exchange their new-found sobriety for their former misery any time they like. No one will stop them. No one can. But sobriety is a powerful drug, and once tasted, few recovering alcoholics ever want to change it for the pain and misery of the suffering alcoholic.

Family meetings are held regularly at the clinics and, when patient, family and counsellor get together to discuss what progress is being made, and also to discuss resentments, angers, hopes and ambitions, nothing but good can come from such meetings. Things that have been hidden for so long are now out in the open and that is no bad thing when dealing with a condition that has all but destroyed that family unit. Private clinics are now an accepted part of alcoholism recovery and no one is more delighted than AA that this is so. Anything that helps the alcoholic to recover is to be welcomed.

Psychiatric Treatment

The chances are that the drinker has already seen the family doctor before moving on to the consulting room of the psychiatrist; and it may well be that he has been completely honest with the doctor (as far as the illness will allow) about his drinking habits. But even if he has not been entirely honest, it won't take long before the regular sessions with the psychiatrist show the truth.

The main function for the psychiatrist now is to try to determine *why* his patient is drinking the way he does; the theory being that if the reasons can be determined, then the patient, in the light of that knowledge, will be able either to stop drinking or at least have some sort of control over the stuff. Sounds good. It should work. But does it?

It is a well-known fact that although it is known how a woman gets pregnant, that knowledge in no way alleviates the condition. And in the same way, a knowledge of just why a person started drinking to excess in no way enables him to regain the control he may have had before the excessive drinking started.

But it would be wrong to minimize the help that can be derived from psychiatry; in his probing for the reasons, the psychiatrist helps to make the patient aware of much of his true self. He helps unravel the phoney world that the alcoholic has probably been living in for years, and his questions and his interpretations of the answers can help the patient to see himself as he really is. The patient may well be immature in many ways, and this will soon be apparent to him. If there is a sincere desire on the part of the patient to improve as a person, and he is prepared to work in close and sympathetic liaison with the psychiatrist, then great benefit can be derived to help eliminate many of the problems that beset him.

The trouble is that when the psychiatrist (rather like the one in the clinic) is getting near to the heart of the problem, and is beginning to hear his patient's innermost thoughts, the wily illness of alcoholism merely 'goes to ground' in the deepest recesses of the victim's mind and waits for the treatment to come to an end. When the patient is discharged — presumably 'cured' — our old foe merely arouses himself from his temporary slumber, has a look round to see where the weakest chink in the victim's armour is, and either sends out a mental invitation to have a glass of that which cheers, or drops the subtlety and attacks with the ferocity of a tiger. It can cause a person who has had prolonged psychiatric treatment and who hasn't had a drink for months to walk into a bar and order a drink. Ask them why they did this seemingly insane thing and the chances are that they will be unable to come up with anything better than 'I didn't think one would hurt me.'

Specialized Hospital Treatment

It may not be widely known but there are hospitals which do specialize in the treatment of alcoholism. The doctors and staff are trained to help the patient back to normality, and it is to their credit that they do so without criticizing or condemning their charges. These devoted helpers see their patients as sick people in the grip of a frightening illness, and they understand a mode of behaviour that would not — could not — be tolerated in any other hospital. When alcoholics are admitted to a hospital of this nature, they are soon aware of this understanding, and it is not long before the majority of them respond to it. To be in an environment where there is no criticism or resentment of their former behaviour is something that is usually new to them, and that in itself must help in their recovery.

But first things first. How does a suffering alcoholic get into one of these hospitals? Sad to say, there are not very many of them around. So the patient who needs specialized hospital treatment will be fortunate if he lives in a district or town where such hospitals are situated.

Assuming that a hospital of this nature is available, he will normally need a letter from his own doctor, stating that he needs the special care and recommending admittance. There may be a waiting list, and the alcoholic may have to 'sweat it out' until a place is available for him. He may, of course, not be able to sweat it out, and it is not unusual for the alcoholic to be admitted to the hospital unit suffering from the effects of his illness, i.e. drunk.

But once admitted to the unit, the patient is in a different world. For a start, the doctors and nurses *know* why he is there. The time for kidding and the pretence is now over (at least as far as they are concerned). It is possible that the patient himself will still try to proclaim to anyone who will listen to him that he is there for reasons other than his drinking. But he kids no one. And when the doctors, nurses and other patients alike know the truth, it isn't long before the patient himself has to accept the fact, and this admittance is the first step in his recovery.

It is almost unknown for an alcoholic to be admitted to a unit without being in some sort of run-down condition. It's a hundred to one that he will be suffering from a vitamin deficiency; and it is also highly likely that he won't have had a decent night's sleep in quite a while. So, again, it's first things first.

For a start, he goes straight to bed, usually with massive vitamin injections. He may, too, be given sedatives not only to help him sleep but also to get him over the worst of the withdrawals. The 'drying out' period can be made as painless as possible, and many alcoholics have been pleasantly surprised to find that being denied the one thing they thought they needed to keep them going is not as bad as they had anticipated.

Depending on the type of alcoholic he has to deal with, the doctor will determine just what kind of treatment the patient will have. There are many kinds of treatment, but the two most common in use are as follows.

Antabuse: This is a drug given in tablet form that has no harmful effects in itself, but if alcohol is taken on top of the tablet, you are really in a bad way. So patients in units can be given small doses of the drug followed by a small quantity of alcohol, and this should have the effect of letting them know how they will feel if they drink on top of the full tablet. It is a fairly unpleasant way to find out, and not many patients drink after taking their daily tablet. Anything that keeps an alcoholic away from booze is a good thing, and Antabuse has an invaluable part to play in his recovery. If an alcoholic really wants to keep off the stuff, and he takes his daily tablet, then it is possible that he will not drink again.

The snag is, of course, that if he does decide to drink again he merely refrains from taking the tablet for a short time, and the minute that the Antabuse is out of the system (after a few days) . . . bingo!

But while in the unit, Antabuse is but one of the methods used to try and get through to the patients that booze, as far as they are concerned, should be a thing of the past.

Aversion Treatment: This type of treatment is used in many of the specialized units. The theory is that the patient receives an injection of a drug and then drinks some alcohol. The sickness that follows will be of such a nature that he will be put off drink for life. Well, that's the theory. And it *should* work, for there is no doubt that the sickness which follows the 'treatment' is acute to say the least. But drinking alcoholics — especially when 'nearing the end' — know all about being sick. There are not many classes of people who are sicker than the early morning drinker trying to force the first one down!

This kind of aversion treatment, like Antabuse, certainly works for some, and for a long spell, too. But the mental beckoning of alcohol is in many ways equal to the task of making the drinker forget all about the sickness he has experienced. If only the sickness, fears, terrors, tears, anguish and pain could stay fresh in the mind, then what alcoholic in his right senses would ever drink again? But, as stated so many times before, the mental aspect of alcoholism has the capacity to make the alcoholic forget all the past problems; and when an alcoholic forgets what he is and what alcohol does to him, he invariably drinks again.

The Group in Hospital: If an alcoholic is admitted to a unit suffering from vitamin deficiency, there is one other thing he is usually suffering from: the knowledge that most of the people he has been close to, i.e. family, friends and colleagues, consider him to be nothing more than a weak-willed, uncaring and selfish drunk. He can't argue too much with this assessment of his character; as far as he is concerned they are probably right. He is invariably ashamed, bitter and resentful at the state in which he finds himself, and at first it is no consolation to know that the other twenty or so people in the unit are in exactly the same position. But once the initial 'drying out' period is over, he can take stock of his position and of his companions, and he soon finds out that, in the main, they are not weak-willed, uncaring and selfish people. They are as sick and as confused as he is, and they too cannot understand just how they came to be in the position they are in.

When they are told by the doctors, nurses and older members of the group that they are in fact suffering from some strange illness, they may not accept this straightaway. But gradually they will come to accept the fact — at least, most of them do — and they will be all the happier and contented with their new-found knowledge.

There will be daily meetings at which the patient will not only get to know his fellow patients — men and women — but will also get to know himself a lot better than he ever did before. As the barriers and the facades are lowered, a bit of the real person emerges, and sometimes an awareness of what alcohol has done to him becomes apparent. Probably for the first time in his life he will admit to the fact that booze is the real cause of his being where he is, and when the fact is admitted, real progress can be made towards recovery. There will be a 'life story' to be written and read to the group — and there are no keener spotters of the phoney than those for whom the phoney way of life was a normal pattern for so many years.

At first there may be resentment as the facade is torn aside, but soon the alcoholic welcomes the honesty of his position. It has probably been so long since he talked or acted with any degree of honesty that he finds the situation acceptable. He starts to become aware that he is actually living without booze (something he thought he could never do) and is starting to enjoy it. And the fact that everyone else is enjoying it too makes the whole thing seem so worthwhile. There will probably be weekly meetings of Alcoholics Anonymous held at the unit, and seeing the recovering alcoholics who come along to talk to the group happy, contented and coping with life and all it brings *without booze*, usually makes some sort of impression on him.

A patient in a specialized unit who spends from one to three months with the group, having daily therapy and also the weekly AA meetings will, all things being equal, get sober. And the patient who follows up his discharge from the unit with 'after care' of some nature, has every chance of *staying* sober. But if the patient concerned does not bother with the after care, then it is only a matter of time before the not unattractive first drink springs to mind. And remember: If You Think It, You Drink It. But again there is a snag. The number of places available in hospital units is indeed limited and the waiting lists are lengthy ones. So, is there an alternative to a long wait for a hospital place? The answer, thankfully, is yes.

9.

HOW TO STAY STOPPED

Some of the world's greatest achievements have been brought about by an inspired thought. Fleming noticed the contaminated culture plate lying in his laboratory, and followed it through to discover penicillin. The law of gravity was first brought to a certain Mr Newton's attention by his idle observation of an apple falling from a tree; and, so we are told, Watt's gazing at the lid of a kettle being forced upwards by the pressure of steam led to the invention of the modern steam engine.

In much the same way, the 'thought' of a certain gentleman named Bill, who was lying in a hospital recovering from the effects of uncontrolled drinking, was to lead to the starting of a fellowship that is remarkable as it is unique. That fellowship is Alcoholics Anonymous.

As Bill lay there in that hospital, desperate for a way out from the pain and misery of his drinking, he had a feeling that if he could get sober, the best way for him to *keep* sober was to help other alcoholics.

A few months later, when Bill had managed to get off the stuff, he found a man who was as desperate as he had been to find a solution to his seemingly impossible task. They met, talked — and that was the first meeting of AA.

This was in the town of Akron, U.S.A., the year 1935, and AA members in their thousands have blessed the day that Bill and Bob had that historic meeting.

Soon there were a hundred members, then a thousand. At the present time there are countless thousands who owe their sanity and their lives to the almost magical workings of AA.

How Does AA Work?
What does it have that the other treatments do not have? Does

the 'cure' last? Three good questions — let's see if we can come up with three equally good answers.

It is one of the facts of life that in certain circumstances combined strength is greater than that of individual effort. So when someone walks through the doors of AA, he is met with the combined strength of people who have been in exactly the same position as the newcomer. The new member gets no sermons, homilies or criticism for behaviour which, in the past, has been condemned by all around them. He or she gets the understanding that can only come from others who have been in exactly the same boat, or bar.

It is not long before the great majority of newcomers respond to this welcome and refreshing change of attitude; and they soon realize that not only are they not unique but that they are, to their fellow members, an 'open book' as far as their drinking goes. The time for kidding has to stop, and they are in the right place to start the journey back to sane, rational and sober living. They really do start to accept the fact that they are not bad people trying to get good, but sick people trying to get well.

It soon becomes apparent that if these other people can get sober, then there is every chance of him making it too. One of the most powerful and effective weapons in the drinking alcoholic's armoury, especially when confronted by doctors, psychiatrists, etc., is the phrase, 'but you don't understand'. This, of course, is partly true; the alcoholic himself doesn't understand. He really believes that it is virtually impossible for either the medical profession or his Church, or both, to fully appreciate just why he must have a drink to keep functioning — even if he is now not functioning! He is not telling lies when he says 'you don't understand'. He really believes that. And because he believes it, all the well-meant, sincere and expert advice is largely wasted on him.

But at an AA meeting he cannot use that particular phrase, and because of that he is deprived of one of his most powerful and telling arguments — or, if you prefer, excuses for drinking. Here they *do* understand, and he knows they understand. His every reason and excuse for drinking is not only understood but has already been used by the ex-tipplers. They are world authorities when it comes to why they should drink, but they are also world authorities when it comes to the reasons why they should not drink.

The Same Problems

If the newcomer has had family troubles, so have they. If he has had job problems, so have they. If he has had hospital treatment, so have they. And if he has had gaol 'treatment', so have they. If he hid bottles, they, too, were adept at this form of subterfuge. If he didn't hide bottles and only drank the finest wines and brandies, so did they. If he drank because he was lonely, sad or inadequate, so did they. And if he drank because the stuff made him gregarious, happy and fulfilled, so did they. If he tries to tell them that his reason for drinking is unique, it will flatten him to hear that many of the members drank for exactly the same reason that he did. If he gets infuriated with the meeting and storms out, they will understand and welcome him back the following week should he care to go.

They will tell him, and keep on telling him, that the reason he now drinks is because he is suffering from a strange illness that is triggered off by the first drink. He may argue, shout, plead or simply stay quiet, but if he sticks around the meetings long enough, he will discover that he is in no way different from his fellow members, that he does have something wrong with him, and that he is not just a moral weakling with no backbone or moral fibre.

Now the strange thing is this: if he does stick around the meetings, he will discover that the people who got sober and managed to stay sober, are the ones who he sees continually at the meetings. So the link between meetings and continued and happy sobriety is certainly no coincidence.

The Perfect After Care Service

The second question was 'What does it have that the other treatments do not have?', and the answer isn't difficult to come up with. Whatever treatment one has had in the past, AA is the perfect 'after care' service. As we have seen, many alcoholics have managed to get sober with the help they received from their doctors, hospitals, psychiatrists, etc. — but their problem was not so much getting sober as *staying* sober. Once away from the confines and the environment of the ward or consulting room, they are faced with the old pressures that were of such magnitude before they went for treatment, and, as stated previously, if the mental side of the illness hasn't been dealt with, the chances are that, sooner or later, the first drink will seem an attractive proposition. Even if the mental side has been dealt with, it must be a continuing process. It is rather like the diabetic who must have daily insulin. It is not much use him having a dose on the Monday and deciding to give the Tuesday a miss. If he adopted that routine, he would be dead in a very short time. In the same way, the alcoholic who is susceptible to the mental side of the illness will have to see this aspect of his complaint constantly, otherwise he is apt to forget just what he is — and the alcoholic who forgets what he is, is heading for a fall. Or a drink!

It is this *constant* reminder aspect that gives AA its success rate.

Immediate Contact

It would be true to say that if an alcoholic was discharged 'cured' by hospital, clinic or whatever, and he could maintain regular contact with the 'after care' service afforded by the particular therapy, there is no reason why he should not stay sober. But, of course, not all hospitals and clinics can possibly afford the time or the staff to maintain a regular contact with former patients; and it is this gradual loss of contact that starts to 'isolate' the alcoholic, and in that isolation the illness of alcoholism breeds fast indeed.

But the alcoholic who is a member of AA can, if he feels like a drink, make almost immediate contact with AA or with another member. This has the effect of 'neutralizing' the craving for a drink; and many indeed are the alcoholics who have been spared the horrors of yet another disastrous drinking bout by the simple act of picking up the phone. But even if a member of AA *doesn't* feel like a drink, the best way to maintain that frame of mind is to stick to the meetings. Members of AA who have been happily sober for years state categorically that although they may have managed to *get* sober, it is only their constant attendance at meetings that *keeps* them sober.

It may be that the thought of having to attend AA meetings for the rest of one's life will not go down too well with certain individuals. Well, as soon as anyone gets fed-up with attending meetings, they can 'resign' at a minute's notice. They don't have to tear up their membership card — there isn't one. They don't get any refund of subscription — there wasn't any. And they have no need to ask that their name be taken off the members' list — there isn't one. When they say that they are 'out', they are out. And when they say that they are 'in', they are in.

Does the 'Cure' Last?

As for the third question, 'Does the "cure" last?', again the answer is simple. It lasts as long as the members wants it to last. In other words, if an alcoholic comes to AA to get sober, he can, if he practises the suggested programme of recovery, put himself in a position whereby he need never drink again if he doesn't want to.

In the past, he may have been dry (and that means merely doing without alcohol), but now he is sober (and that means that he doesn't need alcohol, and *enjoys* not needing it). When an alcoholic starts to enjoy his sobriety, booze plays a smaller and smaller part in his life. As the illness of alcoholism is progressive when the alcoholic is drinking, so the state of sobriety is also progressive when the alcoholic is not drinking.

So it will be seen that AA is not merely a club for drunks, ex or otherwise. It is a fellowship of people who have got together to help share their experiences and to help not only themselves to recover from alcoholism, but also others. It is a collection of 'experts' in the ancient art of drinking. They know all about booze — how to drink it and how not to drink it!

They give hope where there is hopelessness; strength where there is weakness; and knowledge where there is ignorance. Truly, a remarkable fellowship that shows that the alcoholic *needn't* suffer from the illness of alcoholism.

The Mirror of AA

> O was some Power the giftie gie us
> To see oursels as ithers see us!

When Scotland's national poet Robert Burns wrote the above lines, he could well have had AA in mind, for when a member looks into the metaphorical 'mirror' of AA, they see themselves as they really are — warts and all. It can be a painful experience. There, staring them in the face are the lies, deceits, rubbish and nonsense that have been part of their drinking lives for so long. But if AA were merely a mirror to show the new (and sometimes older) member his or her faults, it is also there to show how to put those faults to right.

Four years after the first meeting of AA, a book was published that had been written by the members, and this is entitled *Alcoholics Anonymous,* but known with affection by AA members as The Big Book. In it are the experiences of the founder members and the suggested steps to help people recover from the ravages of alcoholism.

These steps are known as The Twelve Steps. It should be stressed, and it cannot be stressed too strongly, that they really are *suggested* steps, there are no 'musts' in AA. The writers of The Big Book prefaced the Steps with the words, 'If you want what we have . . . Here are the Steps we took . . .' In other words, if you want what they have (happy sobriety) then here is what *they* did to achieve that state. If you do what they did, the chances are that you, too, will achieve happy sobriety. Here are the Steps they took.

1. We admitted we were powerless over alcohol, that our lives had become unmanageable.
2. Came to believe that a Power greater than ourselves could restore us to sanity.
3. Made a decision to turn our will and our lives over to the care of God *as we understood Him*.
4. Made a searching and fearless moral inventory of ourselves.
5. Admitted to God, to ourselves and to another human being the exact nature of our wrongs.
6. Were entirely ready to have God remove all these defects of character.
7. Humbly asked Him to remove our shortcomings.
8. Made a list of all persons we had harmed and became willing to make amends to them all.
9. Made direct amends to such people wherever possible, except when to do so would injure them or others.
10. Continued to take personal inventory and when we were wrong promptly admitted it.
11. Sought through prayer and meditation to improve our conscious contact with God *as we understood Him,* praying only for knowledge of His will for us and the power to carry that out.
12. Having had a spiritual awakening as a result of these Steps, we tried to carry this message to alcoholics, and to practice these principles in all our affairs.

It is not surprising that many new members (many older ones, too) shake their heads at the seeming impossibility of the efforts asked of them. 'This is for saints', is a common retort when faced with the prospect of carrying out such a daunting task. However, the writers of the Steps had already seen this problem and their assertion that 'We are not saints . . .' made it clear that they themselves could but do their best to carry out the suggested task. But their trying brought results that exceeded their wildest dreams. It also exceeded the wildest dreams of their nearest and dearest!

Alcohol

It is interesting to note that the word 'alcohol' is used only once in the Twelve Steps. This surprises many people as it is natural to assume that any writings on the subject of alcoholism would include the word alcohol a few times at least, but there is a reason for this.

When the writers of The Big Book shared their experiences prior to the actual writing of it, they realized that their stopping drinking was only the first step on a long and at times difficult road to recovery from alcoholism. Step 1, therefore, was the foundation stone upon which the other eleven were built and only that step need mention alcohol.

It is impossible to take any of the other Steps until that of Step 1 has been accepted and acted upon, and the alcoholic who takes Step 1 (stops drinking) and then tries as best as he or she can to follow the other Steps must, without doubt, emerge from the experience a much more mature person. So, Step 1 deals with alcoholism, the suffering of; Steps 2 to 12 deal with alcoholism, the Recovery of. As a member once said: I came to AA as a drunken fool, stopped drinking and found that I was no longer a drunken fool — I was a sober fool. The Steps will change all that.

The God Factor

The word 'God' has caused problems for people who would like to have become AA members but just cannot accept the God factor. How is it possible for either an atheist or agnostic to become a member of this Fellowship when they cannot, in all honesty, accept the principle of the Steps that mention God? Again, it was the wisdom of the founders of AA that prompted them to make the Steps 'suggested' ones. AA has many atheists and agnostics amongst its members and when the question is asked how they reconcile their views with the Steps, one can only say that atheists and agnostics arrive as drunken members and finish up as sober ones. But it should be said that when a person starts to mature in AA, changes do take place. When lies, deceits, 'cover ups', violence, intolerance and resentments give way to their new way of life, many members find that they are drawn to 'deeper' thoughts and that their former beliefs are changing (sometimes against their will) towards those of a higher nature. This is why the words 'God *as we understood Him*' are stressed.

Ask any AA member who has been a member for any length of time what, in their opinion, is the most important aspect of AA's teachings, and they will probably answer you with the words of the preamble reading that precedes their meetings: 'Our primary purpose is to stay sober and help other alcoholics to achieve sobriety'. If one achieves sobriety in AA, that is the primary aim. If one also finds God, then that is a bonus that can only be described as priceless. That so many have done so is without doubt.

Many AA members have found that they prefer the words 'Higher Power' to that of the word God. As the Bard of Avon wrote 'A Rose By Any Other name. . . .'

It Gets Better

AA has many little sayings that are designed to help the now-recovering alcoholic make that once difficult road a much easier one to walk.

'First Things First', 'Easy Does It', 'Live And Let Live' are but three sayings that decorate the walls of AA meetings. One of the most useful to the newcomer is the one that reads 'It gets better'. It may well be that, although they have stopped drinking, things don't seem to be all that good for them. There can still be problems at home; it is possible that, although they may have stopped pouring the stuff down their throats, the spouse still has inner resentments and anger at the state the home is in owing to the years of drinking once 'enjoyed' by the now-sober partner. Partners do not always respond immediately to the person who, for possibly years, has caused such turmoil in the home.

Partners are, of course, more than happy that the drinking — and lies, excuses and unkept promises — have now ceased, but they cannot forget the pain that those things have done to them and they find it almost impossible to respond in a manner that the ex-drinker might want or expect. It does take time. All the AA member can do is

1. Stay Sober
2. Make Amends
3. Easy Does It.

If time is taken to put things right that have taken possibly years to put wrong, then it *gets better.* But remember, AA members are not immune to the problems of every-day living. Just because a person has stopped drinking, it does not mean that all will be well.

Every AA member will, at one time or another, experience some kind of a problem in their lives. So, what gets better? When trouble rears its ugly head to the AA member who is sober, what gets better *is the ability to cope.*

When Things Get Worse
Should life decide to hand you the occasional bag of lemons, you have a choice as to what you can do with them:
1. suck them and cry
2. take them home and make some lemonade.

When you decide to adopt the latter option, you are indeed on the road to recovery.

One Day at a Time
It is remarkable that the members of AA who wrote the Big Book could fill it so full of wisdom; remember, they themselves had only been sober for four years. One perfect example is their philosophy of living 'one day at a time'. This, of course, is not a new way of thinking, but AA lived it to such an extent, it became synonymous with the Fellowship.

They discovered that the human mind will accept an instruction for a period of one day that it would totally reject if asked to accept it for a lifetime. So, they took a decision each morning upon waking: just for today I will not have a drink.

They found that they could cope with that and, if followed faithfully, those 'days' turned into 'years'. Ask any AA member who has been sober for some time: 'How long have you been off the booze?' and the chances are that they will tell you, 'I haven't had a drink today.' If it is really relevant to give an exact number of days or years, they will do so. Many AA members have little badges pinned to their clothes with the number of years sober. It is not unusual, especially in America, to see a badge with 10, 11 or whatever number is appropriate on it. But the philosophy is the same. No AA member would ever dream of saying, 'I will never drink again.' They will probably say, 'I hope I have had my last drink', but that is as far as it goes.

The sense of this philosophy can be seen by looking at the example of people who make New Year's Resolutions: millions make them and millions break them. The reason so many people fail to keep to their intentions is because they invariably make the decision to keep their resolutions for *life*. If they adopted the 'one day at a time' philosophy, the chances of success would be all the greater.

Why AA is 'Anonymous'

Many people have asked the question, 'Why is AA anonymous? Is it because they are ashamed or embarrassed by their condition?' Good questions and, remembering the courage of Betty Ford, they deserve good answers.

When AA was first formed in 1935, the members realized that, although they themselves were sober, their illness — alcoholism — was looked upon by 99 per cent of the population as a disgusting and degrading weak-willed condition. They also realized that most people would refuse any form of help that might reveal their identity. So, in its wisdom, AA offered the newcomer the one thing that might entice them to seek the help they so desperately needed — anonymity. All a person needs when they walk, stagger or fall through the doors of AA is a name — a first name will do, and they can use any one they like!

This reason alone would justify anonymity but, as time went on and the number of members grew, they also discovered something else; they discovered that one word kept creeping into their vocabularies, and that word was *ego*. They found that their ego had played as much havoc with their mental selves as alcohol had done with their physical selves. And what is the finest antidote to ego? Anonymity. If you do a good turn and can tell no one about it, then the ego is being deflated or humbled almost without your knowing it. If only the recipient of your 'goodness' knows about it, then ego has no chance to grow.

Every religious order in the world has a method of dealing with the danger of inflated egos, and AA found that anonymity is the most effective in every way for them. Seldom has an organization commanded the respect and affection to the extent that AA has, and when you think that you are dealing with people like John, Mary, Charlie, Eve and Bill, who want no thanks, credit, publicity or money for their help, you will see just why that respect and affection is so well merited.

Supreme Player of the Waiting Game

So, does a person have to stick with AA for the rest of his or her life? The answer is, of course, no, you don't *have* to. However, those who do become sober in AA and then decide to 'go it alone' face a danger that is as dangerous as a waiting cobra — alcoholism.

We know that the mental side of the condition never really goes away. It is in the mind in exactly the same way that every other experience a person has lived through is there — it can never be entirely eliminated and it is the supreme player of the waiting game, it waits for the unwary. It will wait for years and the moment an alcoholic lowers his or her guard, it strikes. Even after years there can be an overwhelming compulsion to take that first drink. Or it may come as a fleeting thought, 'One wouldn't harm me'. When that thought leads to the first drink being taken, you then have, not only a mental obsession, but also a physical compulsion — an unholy alliance that many alcoholics have found out to their cost in a moment of weakness.

And what is the cost? If the cost were to be merely money, then many alcoholics who today are sober would still be drinking. But the cost is much more than money and, as they say, when your drinking costs more than money, you have a problem. AA is the answer not only to the first drink but also the first think. If you think it, you drink it.

It is a fact that patients who have been admitted to a clinic are amazed at the fact that after a short time the desire to have a drink seems to have disappeared. A few days previously, they were at the stage where they couldn't live with it and they couldn't live without it. Then the thought of a drink becomes anathema to them — they can't really understand how they got into the state they did. They complete the course, come out — and are drinking within days.

How can this be? The fact is that they totally underestimated their wily adversary. It really isn't their fault, the 'enemy' was far too strong for them. They will need a 'defence system' that they can call upon at any given moment and there can be no finer system than that offered by AA.

Some may feel disheartened at this. They may think that it will be a life-time struggle against the 'enemy' but this is not so. Once the AA philosophy has been accepted in its entirety, it gets to the stage where the thought of a drink just never enters one's head. But if it should, then the 'defence system' is brought into play and the thought is dealt with immediately. Again, it needs to be said, if the clinic gets you sober, AA keeps you sober. Between the two, you need never drink again. There is a hard way and an easy way to do this and the easy way is, of course, one day at a time.

10.

WHEN THE FAMILY SHOUT 'HELP'

Al-Anon
It has been said that no one suffers more than the alcoholic who
is still drinking — especially as the illness progresses. This is only
partly true. It may well be that no one suffers *more*, but there
is one unit that suffers just as *much* and that is the family of the
drinker.

For so long, maybe years, they have watched the person they
once loved (maybe still do) change from a Jekyll into a frightening
Hyde and, to make it worse, they are never really sure which of
the two is going to walk or fall through the door next. One minute
the drinker is happy, the next he or she is sinking into a sea of
self-pity. At times there is instant laughter, at times there is instant
depression. There can be immediate kindness, then there can
be immediate cruelty, either by deed or by word. It is no wonder
that the partner or family in such a situation often despairs of
either help or solution to what is a seemingly intractable problem.
This despair can also be felt by friends and colleagues of the
problem drinker, for no matter how hard they try to resolve the
problem things seem to be getting worse. The fact is that they
are getting worse.

So, is there anything that can be done in such a situation? Is
there anyone the family and friends can turn to when an alcoholic
will not, or cannot, stop drinking? Thankfully, the answer is 'yes'.
There is help available, and that help is an organization that is,
in its own way, as remarkable as is AA — Al-Anon.

If we go back to the early days of AA, when those first few
members met to discuss their common problem, some of the
men (the first members were all male) would take their wives
along. It was only natural that the wives concerned would talk
with each other about *their* problems, the problems that had been

caused by the years of drinking by their now-recovering partners, and this was really the start of Al-Anon.

As the numbers grew, so did the need for the wives to have their own meeting place to continue their discussions. They found that their suffering was every bit as much as their partner's had been, and to talk this out with 'fellow sufferers' was a tremendous relief. When AA got its first female member, it was only natural to assume that the lady's husband was in the same boat as the lady Al-Anon members. His suffering had been every bit as much as that of his alcoholic wife, and soon Al-Anon was an organization of men and women, sharing their common problems.

Many people think that if the alcoholic stops drinking, then that is the end of the matter. Nothing could be further from the truth. It's a bit like saying that because the bull in the china shop has stopped charging, everything is now fine. But what about the mess that's been left?

When an alcoholic stops drinking, there is usually one gigantic mess to be found. And most of it is often of an emotional nature. During the years of drinking, harsh things have been said and done and, just because the drinking has stopped, it does not mean that the hurt of those years can be washed away by a few wipes of the cloth — the slate may take a lot more cleaning that that. This is where the Al-Anon meetings are invaluable: they help the non-alcoholic partner (or friend or relative) not only to understand the nature of the illness, but also help the partner learn to live with the alcoholic, who may still be drinking. This would seem to be an almost impossible task to accomplish, but they do it. And do it better than any other organization.

Changed Attitudes

Just how *does* one learn to live with a partner whose drinking may slowly (or quickly) be getting worse? This is where Al-Anon proves invaluable. They help the drinker's partner to adopt *changed attitudes* to the whole problem.

The chances are that, in the past, the only way the non-drinking partner (or social-drinking partner) dealt with it was to shout, scream, rage, cry, plead, argue, fight, cower, run away (not always possible) and a dozen other methods that were meant to try and change the drinker's insane behaviour. Their failure certainly wasn't for the want of trying!

Al-Anon teaches them that they *cannot* change the drinker's pattern. It will also teach them that they are not responsible for the drinking, nor are they responsible for the hoped-for recovery. But it will teach them what they *are* responsible for. They are responsible for the way they live their own lives amidst the mayhem of the home. They will be shown that the 'covering up' has got to stop, that the consequences of the drinker's behaviour will have to be brought home to the drinker in all their awfulness. The alcoholic who has created such mayhem the night before will have to awake to the mess that he or she created. The attitude may well have to be 'Drink if you must, but you will now face the consequences of your drinking.' Hard-hearted? No, it's called Tough Love.

In the same way that AA members go to their meetings, Al-Anon members go to theirs: to 'grow' as people. When a new member arrives at Al-Anon, that person is usually at his or her wits end as to what to do. The very first thing the new member is offered is the knowledge that their plight is fully understood, they are not alone. The next thing they are offered is the 'strength' of the meeting. And for someone who walks into that meeting completely drained of all energy, that strength is like an injection of adrenalin.

Al-Anon has adopted the Steps of AA and, because of this, their members go through the same stages of alcoholism recovery as does the drinking (or ex-drinking) partner. A home that has been spiritually (or morally) bankrupt for years needs *both parties* on the recovery programme and Al-Anon is as valuable to the alcoholic's partner as AA is to the alcoholic. When both organizations are used to the full, the end product is remarkable.

There are now nearly 1,000 Al-Anon meetings held regularly in the UK and Eire each week, so never again need those close to an alcoholic shout 'help' and that plea go unanswered.

Alateen

If alcoholics have cause to be grateful to AA, and their partners to Al-Anon then, without doubt Alateen (a part of Al-Anon Family Groups) is invaluable to the children of alcoholics who have reached their teen years and are then in a position to decide just what attitude to adopt to their problem. There is no doubt that a child who has been brought up in the environment of an alcoholic home does indeed have problems.

Many decide that the moment they are of age, they will leave home. They may feel sorry for the non-alcoholic parent, but if they feel that they have 'had enough' of the troubles they have experienced over the years, then they can't be blamed for wanting to leave it all behind the moment they are able.

If they are fortunate enough to find Alateen, however, then they will start to learn that their drinking parent isn't just a drunken oaf who has caused nothing but heartache in the home; they will learn that alcoholism is really a form of illness and, in accepting that fact, they will be able to rethink the whole situation and act accordingly. They too will be able to change their attitudes to the home-life and, when the recovery of both teenager and the non-drinking partner is manifest in the home, *whether the alcoholic is drinking or not*, their life will be lived in a manner that they never thought possible. And when an alcoholic who *is* drinking is presented with a family that seems to avoid all the 'traps' that the alcoholic has previously set for them, it is possible that the changed attitude of the family will prove to be the turning point in his or her thinking. It may take time, it may take a lot more than that for the alcoholic to reach a stage where they have 'had enough' and they want to do something about it, but when they do, it may be that the family will be able to point the way to the drinking partner.

11.

THE NEW YOU

A fool: not so much one who makes mistakes but who repeats them.

Very few people come through the doors of AA on a Brown Ale, and not many people consult their doctor, psychiatrist or any of the other good helpers unless booze is beginning to hurt. If drinking alcohol is a pleasant experience or a tension-relieving necessity, then the drinker probably doesn't have a very great desire to give it up. Why should he? It works.

But when it doesn't work. . . .

And so, when alcohol has done its worst and the time has come to do something about it, the alcoholic is usually at the stage where he'll try anything. But by this time he has probably been drinking for a great number of years. There are, of course, the exceptions. The young alcoholic hasn't had time to spend years acquiring the physical addiction; in some strange way he has managed to get the addiction in a far shorter time than his older brother. Quite a few alcoholics seem to be hooked from the word go, and their social drinking was almost non-existent; it was compulsive tippling from the start.

Filling a Void

However, it usually takes a few years for the 'normal' alcoholic to get to the stage where his drinking starts to show signs of big trouble. And the alcoholic who has been drinking for years and suddenly stops is left with a void that must be filled.

But filled with what?

The alcoholics who achieve sobriety with the help of the medical profession, i.e., doctors, psychiatrists, hypnotists, etc., are usually kept off the stuff either through fear of what will happen should they drink again, or sheer relief that they are at long last freed from the awful compulsion to drink. The fact that they wake up in the morning without the shakes and fears that are the normal accompaniments to drinking is, in itself, enough for this type of alcoholic. The fact that he can actually remember where he has been and what he did the previous night is also a great factor in helping him to keep sober; and if anything else is needed to encourage that happy state of affairs, his wife and family greeting him as some sort of respected person should do the trick.

But that type of alcoholic is the minority. The great majority of alcoholics, even if they manage to get off the stuff, are left with the void that alcohol filled so adequately in years gone by. They are more than happy to be rid of the shakes and the sweats, and they are delighted that they can actually remember the night before — plus the fact that they didn't disgrace themselves by any outrageous behaviour! They welcome the new attitude in the home, and the smile from the wife and the kiss and hug from the children are very acceptable to them. After all, it is a while since they experienced those actions.

But all the time this type of alcoholic is in danger, because he has omitted to do something about the mental aspect of the illness. How could he? He didn't even know there was a mental side. He probably thought, as so many before him have thought, that if an alcoholic gives up drinking alcohol, his problems are over. A dangerous assumption.

Again, we ask the question: 'What replaces alcohol?' The founders of AA, Bill and Bob, made a discovery concerning human behaviour. They discovered that if a person thinks wrongly, then the end product will in some way or another be faulty. So, even if an alcoholic stops drinking, if there are still thoughts in his head that are not compatible with a normal, mature and dignified way of life, he may well revert to drink.

As the thought precedes the action, so thought precedes the drink. And if the thought is in the head of the alcoholic, then sooner or later the first drink will seem an attractive proposition to him.

It must be stated here and now that the thought of drink can never entirely be eradicated from the mind of the alcoholic, just as the thought of any single thing cannot be eradicated from the memory cells. Once it is there, for good or bad, it is there to stay.

Defence Mechanism

So, members of AA do not try to eliminate the thought of the first drink; they know that's impossible. What they do try to do is to surround themselves with such a barrier of defence mechanism that the thought of the drink just cannot get through to them. And if it does get through, then they have a counter thought to combat the drink thought. In other words, they feed the mind with the positive thoughts of sobriety, and if the negative destructive thoughts of a drink 'come through', they have a wall of mental defence to sustain them. As they add to this defence wall, the thoughts of a drink get less and less opportunity to come through, and it is not unusual to hear an AA member who has been sober for some time say: 'I just never think of a drink now.'

But, of course, as the diabetic needs his daily insulin, so the alcoholic needs his daily 'sobriety injection'. The ingredients of this particular injection are: knowledge of the illness, knowledge of the self, awareness of one's character defects, and a willingness (and a method) to do something about them.

A Programme for Staying Sober

Again we return to the remarkable fellowship of AA; for it was the first hundred members — remember, all of them ex-drunks — who devised a programme that will help the man or woman who has stopped drinking, not only to stay sober, but to emerge from it all as a better, bigger and happier human being.

Remember what Burns wrote about 'Seeing ourselves as others see us'? This is exactly what the mirror of AA helps one do. In this mirror the alcoholic sees himself as he really is. Gone are the clothes which helped to create the illusion of grandeur. Exposed to his gaze are the layers of rubbish, nonsense, self-gratification and self-pity that have beset and deluded him for years. For the first time he can see the person he really is — and it usually comes as quite a shock. He isn't the nice guy that he has fondly imagined himself to be. It may be true that his drinking friends have told him what a great character he is, and, being the egoist he is, he is more than happy to believe this. But his wife knows different. And his family and close friends know different. And now *he* is starting to know different.

Once the mirror has done its work and shown him just what he really is, it would be useless to leave him like that. There has got to be something worthwhile to help strip away these layers of delusion and deception which have made it impossible for him to mature as the man he should be. It is not enough to point out the faults — there has to be a remedy for the whole exercise to be worth pursuing in the first place.

When he is aware of these character defects, this very recognition is a tremendous help in overcoming them. As the ego is slowly but surely brought under the deflationary process of the AA way of life, the alcoholic starts to feel the first glimmerings of concern for others; and that is an emotion he probably hasn't experienced for quite a few years. When a person starts to care for the well-being and happiness of his fellow men (and that includes his wife, family, friends and colleagues), there eventually follows a happiness that can only be experienced and not described.

Developing New Values

Once again there is laughter in the home. And once again there is happiness to be shared by all the family. But most important of all, there is love. The word will assume a new meaning for the ex-drinker. In the past, it could only be used in the personal sense: the alcoholic loved himself; at the finish of his drinking, he hated himself. But now there is a love of all around him. It is true that he won't find the company of fools all that easy to keep, as he did in the past, but with his new-found sobriety will come a new tolerance and understanding.

12.

TO SUM UP

This book will have been of value if it does nothing else than help the problem drinker to come to a decision regarding his or her drinking. If it costs the tears of either spouse or children, or any form of unhappiness in the home, then maybe something will have to be done about it. If you *do* decide to do something, you will be among the lucky ones, for it is a sad fact that alcoholism 'claims' so many victims.

Almost every country in the world has an alcoholism problem and all of them are attempting to tackle it in their own way. France, which was known as the home of 'civilized' drinking, where wine with a meal was an accepted part of family life, has one of the highest alcoholic problems in the world. It would appear then that 'teaching' the children how to drink is no guarantee that the problem will not appear in later life.

In countries where the sale of booze has been severely curtailed, the problem of alcoholism is still with them. If people can't buy it, they'll make it! Prohibition was tried in the USA in the thirties and it brought to the fore such characters as Al Capone and his fellow booze-runners. If *you* can't buy it and you can't make it — someone else will! As the saying goes, bad booze is better than no booze — to the drinker. American AA members smile when they hear folks say that the West was won by the Winchester. They know what won the West — whisky. It did far more damage to the Red Indian peoples than ever a bullet from a Winchester did.

The First Step

If you are worried about your drinking and you really want to do something about the problem, you have made the first step on the road to recovery. For the problem drinker who either cannot or will not accept that he has a problem is almost impossible to help. When a person says, albeit grudgingly, 'OK, maybe I do overdo it a bit. What shall I do?' then there is hope of a better life not only for him but for all those around him.

So where do we start? We start with the first drink — try not taking it and do this on a daily basis. Do not make the cardinal mistake of giving up alcohol for life. Remember what was said earlier, that the mind will accept an instruction for one day that it will totally reject if asked to accept it for a lifetime. But if you can't do without a drink and you must have the next one, regardless of the tears, rages and recriminations of others then there are avenues of help.

Hypnotism and Religion
The hypnotist has had his successes, of that there can be no doubt, but if everyone who reads this book were to try hypnotherapy as a means of resolving their drink problem, there just wouldn't be enough practitioners to go around. And even if they did have a certain success, remember what was said about the wily old adversary merely retreating until the treatment is over.

No one on this earth can deny the drinking alcoholic the right to a prayer to the god of his or her choice. They are entitled to that — sometimes that is all they have left. Like the miracles that are reported from such places as Lourdes, there have been cases where the alcoholic has prayed for the obsession to drink to be taken from him — and it has! But, of course, these cases are noted more for their rarity than for their frequency. As for the prayers that the alcoholic will be able to return to social drinking, they are offered in their millions and unanswered in equal numbers. To date, at least according to those who work in close liaison with alcoholics, there has never been a single case of an alcoholic being able to resume social drinking. The fact that so many try to be the first one to accomplish this shows the persuasive powers of alcohol.

Hospital or Special Unit
If alcohol is being drunk to the extent that it is causing either physical or mental problems, then it may be that the alcoholic will simply have to go into either a hospital for 'drying out' or a special clinic, and there can be no doubt whatsoever that the latter is infinitely more effective for this purpose. Special units are geared to alcoholism and there isn't much that the staff do not know about the physical and mental aspects of the illness.

The chances are that if you spend the stipulated time in a special unit — from one to three months — you will return home not only sober, but also with a desire to stay sober.

Staying Sober

And how do you stay sober? The 'after care' service, of course, and this brings us back to AA again. If you want to stay sober, stick with the winners. AA members are presented with a programme of recovery, a suggested programme, not one they are ordered to follow. One of the most important points in the whole recovery programme of AA is that the member keeps away from the first drink for one day at a time.

This guideline ensures that there is no great conflict taking place inside them as to what they are going to do at Christmas time or how they will cope with the office party or their attitude to cousin Winnie's wedding. They live one day at a time and by the time Christmas arrives or the office party is due or cousin Winnie's big day has dawned, it is just another day to the AA member. A very important day, no doubt, but still just another day and one in which booze plays no part in their plans.

There are many good people only too willing to try to help the suffering alcoholic and all have their part to play in his or her recovery. Some want or need to be paid for their services and this is no bad thing. The labourer is, or should be, worthy of his hire. The suffering alcoholic with money is therefore in a better position than the suffering alcoholic without money, at least as far as certain treatments are concerned. But it should be remembered that the success rate of Alcoholics Anonymous stands second to none, and there are no dues or fees to pay. They are entirely supported by their own contributions.

Help From Doctor or Psychiatrist

The family doctor should be a friend as well as your medical adviser and it is perfectly natural that it is to him that you should turn if there is a problem with alcohol. The very fact that you admit that the visit is about alcohol abuse — even if the phrase used is 'my wife thinks I'm overdoing it a bit' — will mean that you won't waste his time or yours by trying to find 'hidden' ulcers or prescribing sleeping tablets and tranquillizers for a troubled mind. He may think he can treat the problem himself and, if you have enough faith that he can in fact do so, it might just work. But there is one thing for sure, if his treatment doesn't work, you'll be the first to know!

Remember, however, that alcoholism is not on the curriculum of any medical school. It may be mentioned briefly at some schools but, in general, most doctors leave medical school with as little knowledge about the subject as they had when they went in. This is not their fault. Hopefully one day the powers that be will see that the subject *is* studied.

If the doctor decides that he is not qualified to deal with this condition, he might suggest that a psychiatrist may be more able to help. If you have money, treatment can be offered almost immediately. The sessions are usually held weekly and last for approximately one hour. If you are not in a position to pay, you can receive treatment from the National Health psychiatrist. Access to this type of therapy is extremely limited and there is a fairly long waiting list. But whether one goes privately or not, decide (if you can) to tell the truth as to why you are there. It may be that the patient will find it impossible to tell the truth, such is the nature of the illness, but a good psychiatrist shouldn't take too long to find out that somewhere along the line, booze is involved. Successes in the treatment of alcoholism have been achieved by this method and, again, it must be stressed that if you do decide on this approach to the problem, be as honest as you can.

At this point a word of warning should be offered. Some psychiatrists — not, I might add, those in special hospital or clinic centres — seem to think that if only they can find out the reason or reasons for the alcoholic drinking the way they do then, by resolving those reasons, somehow, certain alcoholics will one day be able to drink socially again. If a maxim were to be offered to such psychiatrists, then the following one should be printed in letters three feet high above their desks: ALCOHOLICS SHOULDN'T DRINK ALCOHOL.

13.
I WONDER WHAT HAPPENED TO . . .

(Three true case histories)

Geraldine was born in Ireland, and it is doubtful if a more attractive girl ever emerged from the Emerald Isle. She was one of a family of seven, and if a certain event had not taken place when she was sixteen, the chances are that Geraldine, like her three sisters, would now be happily married in the small country town a few miles from Dublin.

But something did happen, and that something was a local beauty contest. Geraldine emerged as the undisputed winner, which led to her photograph appearing in a Dublin newspaper, and it was not long before the young and lovely girl was appearing in beauty contests all over the country. Her success was rapid, and before long she found herself in London, entering and winning yet more contests.

With the world seemingly at her feet, and a host of admiring young men — all of them with money — life had never been better. It was a life of excitement, parties, men — and alcohol.

With her youth and vitality, she was able to take it all in her stride for quite a few years, but slowly the life she was leading began to have an effect and Geraldine found that she was no longer the odds-on favourite to win the contests she was entering, and entering less frequently at that!

Of all the things that she couldn't take, to come nowhere in the running was the bitterest pill of all for her to swallow. And so, to help the bitter pill of disappointment go down, Geraldine made alcohol her ally. Booze, which in the past had been merely a social extra, now became an imperative daily routine, only this time there were no parties and young men with money to keep her company. She was a loner.

It was not all that long before the drinking was completely out of control, and Geraldine made her first appearance in court; the charge was 'drunk and disorderly'. The sheer indignity of this come-down was soon drowned in the comfort of a glass of cheap plonk — and the life of pain, anguish and misery had started for real. She made her first real attempt to break away from the now vicious grip of alcoholism in 1962, and when she was admitted to a special unit for the treatment of the illness everybody sighed with relief.

She was discharged after the usual three months feeling fit, well — and sober.

She kept sober for five months, during which time she got herself a job in one of London's major stores, managed to get a small flat, and acquired a new and genuine circle of friends. Life seemed good. Then she received a telegram from Ireland with the news that her mother had died. Geraldine's grief was genuine, and she relieved it in the only way she knew how: she took a drink.

She was again admitted to the special unit, this time for four months; she was eventually to be admitted six times in all.

During her spells in the unit she attended the weekly meetings of AA (attendance is mandatory in most of the hospitals) and had to listen to the many recovering alcoholics who came along to tell their stories. She hadn't really paid much attention at any of the meetings, but one night she heard a woman speak about her life on the stage and how the lure of the bright lights and all that went with it had led her into the world of the obsessive drinker.

For the first time in months Geraldine was forced to listen for the simple reason that the speaker, Joan, was 'talking her language'. In some strange way she found that she identified with another human being — at least as far as her drinking was concerned.

She and Joan had a talk after the meeting, and Geraldine felt a strange feeling come over her. Was it possible that she, too, could find what Joan had so obviously found? Could she live a life in which alcohol had no place, and sobriety was something to be treasured and not simply endured? She had never thought it possible, but this meeting up with Joan had brought her the first glimmerings of hope.

Geraldine didn't make too many promises as to what she was going to do when she was finally discharged from the unit. But she did promise Joan that she would go along with her to one of the AA meetings. After all, it wouldn't cost her anything, and if she didn't like what she saw and heard, she could always exchange their way of life for her old drinking days.

On going to the meetings, however, Geraldine realized one thing above all others: no matter what happened, even if she did drink again, her drinkings days would never be the same. But the strange thing is that she didn't drink again. In an almost indefinable way she made the exchange: AA for booze. One took the place of the other, and Geraldine found that the swop was a bargain she hadn't anticipated.

She now knows quite a few things that make sense to her. She knows that her beauty queen days are over, but this doesn't seem to have the importance it had before. She knows that if ever she wants to swop the life she now has — a life that includes laughter, happiness and dignity — all she has to do is take the first drink. To date — and it's quite a few months since the last drink — she hasn't thought it worth it.

Tom didn't have to struggle for anything in life, for he had been born into a very wealthy family and had the finest education that money could buy. He left his native Edinburgh when he was twenty-four to come to London and work in one of the big City banks. By the time he was thirty, he was married with two children and held a position of authority at the bank. All seemed to be going his way. He had been drinking socially, especially at the City functions that seem to be part of that way of life, but not enough to worry about.

But as he was given more authority — and consequently more responsibility — he found that his drinking was being stepped up somewhat. He always made an excuse to leave the office just before opening time, and it wasn't unusual to see him hurry into the nearest pub, order two large scotches and down them as quickly as he could. When this performance became too obvious, he took to having the bottle in his office desk, and the moment he felt the tension of his work beginning to manifest, he had the instant solution.

This went on for quite some time, and with no apparent consequences. But the seeds were being sown for future problem fruits, and one day Tom turned up drunk for an important conference. He made all the usual excuses — he had a heavy cold and had taken something for it, must have taken too many aspirins to relieve the headache, and so on — and got away with it.

If Tom had learned his lesson from that, all would have been well. But, of course, he wasn't in a position to learn anything about anything, and before long he again turned up drunk for a very important meeting. This time the managing director told him that this just couldn't go on and he proposed that Tom should seek treatment in a private clinic in North London. There were no money worries, as the clinic's bill would be covered under the private insurance scheme of which all the bank's employees were members; and Tom's salary would be paid in full as long as he was in the clinic.

This seemed an ideal arrangement for all concerned, and all concerned were happy with the deal.

Tom had his 'treatment' in what can only be described as sheer comfort — and when you consider that the bill for the treatment was over £700 per week, it is not to be wondered at. He emerged as a Mark 2 model and was welcomed back at the bank with open arms.

He was back in the clinic again within three months, only this time there were no open arms from the bank, only a polite request that he resign (they were doing him a favour) or he would be sacked.

Tom resigned, but with a very healthy bank account in his name he didn't worry too much about the future. He took his time to determine just what job he would favour with his presence, and within a few weeks he found himself working for one of the largest American firms based in this country. Remembering the fiasco of the last job, Tom took things very easily as far as his drinking was concerned, and both employers and family were delighted with his behaviour and his ability.

This happy state of affairs lasted for a few months until one day — and these are Tom's own words, 'I was walking along the road and I just fancied a drink.' He just fancied a drink! So, he had one. And another. And he found himself back in the same clinic.

This time the resident psychiatrist tried extra hard to find out just why Tom drank the way he did. But whether anything relevant was found out or not, he was discharged after three weeks. After all, he was as sober as the proverbial judge. And when Tom was sober, they just couldn't find anything wrong with him.

It was at this point that Tom made a call to the AA office in London and asked if someone could come round and have a chat to him about the whole problem. That same night a member who lived nearby called on him. They talked for quite a few hours and at the end of it all Tom said that he didn't honestly think that the illness of alcoholism was his problem. He was sure that the cause of his drinking was sheer pressure of work, and if only he could get away from the environment he was in, he would be all right.

The AA member pointed out that what he was proposing was known as a 'geographical change', and that it was well known to those who had tried it that all they did was to change their present 'local' for the one in the new district. But Tom was convinced that if only he could make the change, all would be well. Within a month he had fixed himself up with a job on the Continent at a salary of £10,000 per annum.

He left his wife and children at home while he arranged things, the idea being that he would send for them once he had settled into the job and found a nice new home. All seemed to be going well, except for one thing: one day Tom fancied a drink. And he took it. The result was acute alcoholic poisoning.

He collapsed in the hotel bar and was rushed to hospital where he died without regaining consciousness. Tom had taken that one drink too many. As the saying goes: You can always get another drink, but you may not get another recovery.

Peggy used to count her blessings every day. She was one of the lucky ones who really did appreciate the fact that she had the things that she wanted to make her a happy and contented person. She had a husband whom she loved very much and who loved her in return. Her two children were growing up in just the manner she wanted them to, and she had a comfortable home. It is doubtful if there were any happier families in the Midlands than Peggy's.

She had never wanted to get a job; for her the home was a full-time occupation. She did not find housework a grind; in fact, the opposite was the case. To see the smiles on the faces of her family when they arrived home at night to a warm, clean and well-cared for house was reward enough.

It was indeed a great day when the first of her children was married, and Peggy was happy with her daughter's choice of husband: a nice, steady boy whom she knew would care for and look after her only girl. The only thing that put a bit of a damper on the whole thing was the fact that her daughter would be moving to another town to be near her husband's work. Still, Peggy had her husband and her son, and they were a full-time job.

But it wasn't all that long before the son got married, and when he moved away from the district Peggy realized for the first time how much she had come to depend on her children for her 'company'.

The days seemed to drag on and on, and Peggy found that her boredom was becoming unbearable. One morning after tidying the house — a job that took less and less time these days — Peggy did something she had never done in her life before: she had a morning glass of sherry. And she felt all the better for it. She used to look forward to getting the place tidy each morning so that she could sit and relax with her glass of sherry (the measures were becoming a bit larger each time) and she thought that a glass of sherry was much the same as a cup of tea.

At first Peggy enjoyed the warm glow that came with the sherry, and after letting it do its relaxing work, she would go shopping and finish all the other household jobs. But gradually she found that the tidying up of the house was being done in a manner that her husband did not find acceptable, and the rows when he came home at night were getting more and more bitter.

Peggy was beginning to drink more and one of her biggest problems was trying to get rid of the empty bottles — inconspicuously! She also had to change her off-licence as the knowing looks of the manager were making her feel uncomfortable. It was only when her husband came home one night and found that the housework had not been done, the evening meal had not been cooked, and Peggy was lying dead drunk on the couch with two empty sherry bottles that the bewildered man decided to call the doctor.

The doctor was rather annoyed at being called out to 'just a drunk' and told Peggy to pull herself together. Peggy made strenuous efforts to do just that, whilst at the same time making equally strenuous efforts to drink two bottles of sherry a day without it showing. Needless to say, it couldn't be done. Peggy's shame, guilt and remorse were as real as the off-licence's bills, and when she attempted to commit suicide, she was admitted to hospital. Again she was told to act her age, be more responsible, find new interests, and was then sent home. For a few months, she tried desperately to recreate her interest in the home, but slowly the boredom returned, and with it came the awareness that she had, at her finger tips, the instant solution to boredom — booze. On finding his wife lying drunk on the couch yet again, Peggy's husband phoned AA in sheer desperation. 'Come and get my wife sober,' was the cry. The man at the other end of the line smiled sadly. If only he could. If he could *give* sobriety away there wouldn't be another human being suffering from alcoholism ever again. But, of course, he couldn't give it away. It must be sought after and, in the strange manner of non-understanding, it must be desired. 'Does your wife want us to come and see her?' he asked. Peggy's husband didn't really know the answer to that one, so he asked her. That night two AA members from the local group paid Peggy a visit. They talked for three hours and at the end of it all Peggy made the vow that she would never touch another drop. She said that she wouldn't bother to come to the meeting as she was now convinced that she could say 'No more' and stick to it.

The two AA members left their telephone numbers and told her to give them a ring if ever she needed them. Peggy used all her willpower and determination and stuck it out for three weeks. Then one day she decided that 'just one' wouldn't hurt her. Her husband called the numbers he had been left and again Peggy sat in her armchair, shaking and hearing that 'it's the first drink that does the damage'.

Again she made the vow 'Never again', and this time it lasted for a month. She felt fit, well and bored; a fairly dangerous trinity, and one to which a fourth is invariably added. The fourth in this case was a bender that had Peggy at the stage where she just couldn't stop drinking, and she carried on until she finally collapsed.

This time she listened to the two AA members with different ears. This time she finally realized, deep down, that her problem was just too big for her to tackle on her own. This time she was determined at least to give the meeting a try.

She didn't find it easy, but then none of the members had found it easy. She stuck with it, and slowly the change in the thinking took place. Boredom gave way to interest; an interest that made Peggy grow and mature as a person.

Today she has a choice as to whether she drinks or not — something she never had before, for when Peggy thought of a drink in the past, there was no choice, only compulsion. To date, Peggy chooses not to drink and thinks that the benefits are worth it. So does her husband, and her two children and five grandchildren who now look forward so eagerly to their regular visits. They find it good to 'come home' to Mum. Their visits are no longer a duty, but a pleasure.

ON WHICH STEP ARE YOU?

Light social drinking
Moderate social drinking
Heavy social drinking
Rows and arguments
Need for the first drink
Excuses made for drinking
Memory blackouts
Promises and attempts to control
Fail to control
Promises and attempts to stop
Fail to stop
Change of house, district, etc.
Family and social life in chaos
The 'shakes' and the early morning drink
Neglect of proper diet
Secret drinking
Continually 'topped' up
Can't live without it — can't live with it
Complete defeat admitted
Uncontrolled drinking
HELP!

Freedom
Help other alcoholics to get sober
Others start to enjoy your sobriety
You start to enjoy your sobriety
Do what must be done
Personal stock-taking
New interests gained
Make amends to family, etc.
Self-respect returns
Refuse to 'escape' via alcohol
The old fears start to go
Believe that life CAN
be good without alcohol
Mix with other sober and
contented alcoholics
Learn about the illness
Feel good mentally
Feel good physically
Keep away from the first drink
Know that it is the FIRST drink that does the damage
Accept help

This chart could be added to at length, but one thing is definite: when the 'Help' stage is reached, that is the individual alcoholic's own 'rock bottom'.

SOURCES OF HELP

Alcoholics Anonymous
Here are the addresses and telephone numbers for England and Wales, Scotland, Northern Ireland, Eire and London. A letter or a call to them will give you the address and time of your nearest meeting.

England and Wales
The General Service Board of Alcoholics Anonymous
PO Box 1
Stonebow House
Stonebow
York YO1 2NJ
Telephone: 0904 644026

Scotland
Scottish Service Office
Baltic Chambers
50 Wellington Street
Glasgow G2
Telephone: 041 2219027 — 9.00am to 5.00pm Monday to Friday

Northern Ireland
Central Service Office
152 Lisburn Road
Belfast BT9 6AJ
Telephone: 0232 681084

Eire
Dublin Service Office
109 South Circular Road
Leonard's Corner
Dublin 8
Telephone: Dublin 774809

London Region Telephone Service
01-352 3001 — 10am to 10pm, answering machine at other times

Al-Anon and Alateen
For relatives and friends of problem drinkers.
61 Great Dover Street
London SE1 4YF
Telephone: 01-403 0888 — 10am to 4pm, answering machine
at other other times

ACCEPT (Addictions Community Centres for Education,
Prevention, Treatment and Research)
200 Seagrave Road
London SW6 1RQ
Telephone: 01-381 3155

If anyone reading this book is, at the time of reading it, absolutely
desperate about their drinking problem (or the drinking problem
of someone close to them) and is willing to accept immediate
treatment at a specialized clinic, then a telephone call to one of
the following clinics may help:

Broadreach House
465 Tavistock Road
Plymouth
Devon PL6 7HE
Telephone: 0752 790000

Broadway Lodge
Oldmixon Road
Weston-super-Mare
Avon BS29 9NN
Telephone: 0934 812319

Clouds House
East Knoyle
near Salisbury
Wiltshire SP3 6BE
Telephone: 074-783 650, 587 or 655

Galsworthy Lodge
The Priory
Priory Lane
London SW15 5JJ
Telephone: 01-876 8261 or 01-876 6371

St Andrews Hospital
Alcohol Treatment Unit
Billing Road
Northampton
Northamptonshire
Telephone: 0604 29696 — answerphone

This is by no means a complete list — for your nearest specialized clinic or NHS hospital with an Alcohol Treatment Unit, call Alcohol Concern who will be able to help you (for their address see page 94).

SOURCES OF INFORMATION

Alcohol Concern
305 Grays Inn Road
London WC1X 8QF
Telephone: 01-833 3471

Greater London Alcohol Advisory Service
91-93 Charterhouse Street
London EC1M 6BT
Telephone: 01-253 6221

The Institute of Alcohol Studies
12 Caxton Street
London SW1H 0QS
Telephone: 01-222 5880

Triple A (Action on Alcohol Abuse)
3rd Floor
11 Carteret Street
London SW1H 9DL
Telephone: 01-222 3454

INDEX